THE
GREAT
AMERICAN
BOMB
MACHINE

Books by Roger Rapoport

IS THE LIBRARY BURNING? (WITH LAURENCE J. KIRSHBAUM)

THE GREAT AMERICAN BOMB MACHINE

THE GREAT AMERICAN BOMB MACHINE

ROGER RAPOPORT

E. P. DUTTON & CO., INC. | NEW YORK | 1971

Published simultaneously in Canada
by Clarke, Irwin & Company Limited, Toronto and Vancouver

Library of Congress Catalog Card Number: 78-158588
SBN 0-525-11610-9

Portions of this book appeared in different form
in *West* and *Ramparts* magazines.

For Leo Goodman

Acknowledgments

This book would not have been possible without the help given me by Jim Bellows, associate editor of *The Los Angeles Times*. A number of other people were particularly generous with me during the nearly two years I spent on this project. They are John Gofman, Arthur Tamplin, Edward Martell, Paul Jacobs and Herbert York. Major General Edward Giller, Vice Admiral L. M. Mustin, Colonel Ed Huycke, Bruce Hanson and the public-relations offices of the Atomic Energy Commission at Germantown, Bethesda, Albuquerque, Los Alamos, Amarillo and Berkeley also helped me. Some of the research was made possible by a grant from the Fund for Investigative Journalism.

—Roger Rapoport

El Cerrito, California
April 25, 1971

Contents

CHAPTER ONE

FUN WITH FATMAN

Fat Man and Little Boy, Lulu and Bullpup, Honest John and Davy Crockett; these are some of curator Carol Canfield's favorite things. Every time she takes another group of Cub Scouts or school kids through her Sandia Atomic Museum she replenishes her love for these A- and H-bombs that have done so very much to protect the American way of life. They come in whites, grays and greens, and rest on pedestals behind gold ropes. There are little bombs such as the 51-pound Davy Crockett, designed to help infantrymen knock out tanks and bridges. There are big bombs such as MK-17, built for airmen to demolish entire cities.

The children love to touch the sleek metal bodies, sharp fins and compact warheads. They also want to know what the big yellow parachute does for MK-61. Mrs. Canfield answers sweet and low as she has done hundreds of times before: "Why, they slow the descent of the weapon to give the delivery plane time to escape or lay the bomb down for later detonation." And what's this switch over here? "Why, it retracts the tail fin on the MK-17 to make it easier to load and unload. Flip it yourself and see what happens."

Here, under one Albuquerque roof, the Pentagon's Defense

Nuclear Agency displays 38 nuclear bombs, 30 scale models, 12 charts on atomic-bomb history, radiation-detection equipment, underground-testing displays, plus four films on nuclear principles and weapons development, including one for children. Parked outside this onetime warehouse are a couple of nuclear bombers and an atomic cannon. New displays arrive regularly, and someday soon Mrs. Canfield plans to open a museum curio shop that will sell scale models of Fat Man and Little Boy, the nuclear bombs that took care of Hiroshima and Nagasaki: "I know we could sell a lot of them, particularly to the kids and our many Japanese visitors. That would give us money to go out and find more bombs to complete our collection. All these bombs deserve a permanent home. They won our last big war and prevent the next one."

From opening day in October 1969 the Sandia nuclear-bomb museum has rivaled White Sands and the Santa Fe Opera as a leading state tourist attraction. During the first year over 50,000 visitors showed up, forcing Mrs. Canfield to lengthen visiting hours to 9:00 A.M.–5:00 P.M., seven days a week. Visitors have come from every state and over 50 foreign countries. Dignitaries who have taken the tour include the president of Argentina and the entire supreme court of Afghanistan. The guestbook is filled with favorable comments like "good show" or "I particularly enjoyed Fat Man." A few cynics have signed inscriptions like "Venceremos—J. Robert Oppenheimer, Alamogordo, New Mexico."

Aside from minor pranks of this sort, Mrs. Canfield has had no political problems: "We thought we might get picketed when the museum opened but nothing happened." Both the A- and H-bomb sections of the museum are filled with nuclear memorabilia. Among the exhibits is a leaflet prepared for dropping on Hiroshima and Nagasaki: "A message to Japanese citizens. Immediately move from the city and take shelter. Carefully read this leaflet it is of great consequence to you: The allied countries have extended an offer to the military leaders of Japan to accept the conditions of the Potsdam Declaration but they refuse to accept it, therefore Russia has declared war on Japan. The U.S. has invented an atomic bomb as powerful as 2,000 B-29's dropping their bombs all at one time. . . ." Beneath the display is a note from Mrs. Canfield telling visitors: "This leaflet was to be distributed over drop area but was withheld for obvious tactical reasons."

As a member of the state museum association and applicant to the American Association of Museums, this Pentagon unit tries to service community needs. On Armed Forces Day military men can count on a loan of nuclear-weapons exhibits. One local theater asked for a little something to dress up their lobby during the run of the film *2001*. So the museum staff sent over a reentry vehicle and radiation-monitor mannequin dressed in a dashing suit of yellow protective clothing. Even the McDonnell-Douglas Company model club was able to borrow Little Boy and Fat Man models so they could make their own replicas.

Another museum community service is a display, "Effects of Nuclear Explosions." Mounted on one wall is an Albuquerque street map pocked with lights activitated by switches. This is the sort of thing chambers of commerce place in busy urban hotels to help visitors locate important civic landmarks. But on this particular map, activating the various switches shows the perimeter of destruction wrought by hypothetical ten-kiloton and one-megaton nuclear blasts in Albuquerque. By flipping one of four switches visitors can find what either of these bombs would do to reinforced-concrete buildings or wood-frame residential buildings. The display shows a ten-kiloton blast would cause severe damage to all concrete buildings within half a mile and to all wood-frame residential buildings within 1.5 miles. The one-megaton shot would result in severe damage to all concrete buildings within 2.5 miles and to all wood-frame buildings within 5.5 miles. The children love to come and play with this exhibit by the hour. They make a great game of figuring out if their home or their father's office would survive nuclear attack. Occasionally visitors will discover their house is at the ground-zero point and complain about it. Others get mad because their homes fall within the severe-damage area. "They want us to move the bomb over to the other side of town," says Mrs. Canfield. She likes to answer with a film. It shows how our nuclear defense system protects Albuquerque and every other American city from an atomic holocaust. "Nuclear bombs are nothing to fear," says the curator. "They are just another weapon in the arsenal. A hundred years from now, people will look upon them as mere bows and arrows."

CHAPTER TWO

THE MANUFACTURERS

On August 5, 1963, the United States, Great Britain and Russia signed a treaty pledging cessation of atmospheric nuclear weapons testing. The pact, which came after a previous treaty had been broken, was the product of international concern over fallout's deleterious effects on mankind. For over a decade responsible scientists like the late Albert Schweitzer and Linus Pauling had cried that nuclear tests were irreversibly contaminating the biosphere with long-lived fission products. On signing the treaty, the United States claimed it ultimately wanted to discontinue "all test explosions of nuclear weapons for all time, and . . . put an end to the contamination of man's environment by radioactive substances."

The American diplomats put much more than nuclear testing underground with the 1963 treaty. They also buried Americans' worst fears about the nation's nuclear weapons complex. Most Americans forgot about strontium-90, iodine-131, and cesium-137. A crucial national issue dissipated back into the hands of anonymous men who work in obscure places with unfamiliar names like Germantown, Rocky Flats, Pantex and Mercury. These are the men who take responsibility for the design, production, testing, transport, stockpiling, and retirement of tens of thousands of nuclear bombs and warheads at hundreds of locations around the world. With the public appeased by the test ban, they could return their full attention to "tactical" nuclear weapons and "clean" hydrogen bombs. Congress could debate the efficacy of MIRVs and ICBMs. The President could propose developing an ABM system without fear of contaminating the people.

But the simple expedient of putting tests underground has not prevented the American nuclear weapons program from continuing to add toxic radionuclides to the atmosphere. Since 1963 fires, explosions, leaks, ventings, and plane crashes have all released dangerous fission products. From the uranium mines on the Colorado plateau to the nuclear graveyards in the Northwest, the weapons program has left its skull and crossbones. The fact is that today's major nuclear threat to America emanates from Washington, not Moscow or Peking. Mindless design, production, testing and transport of nuclear weapons may be a greater threat to national security than all our enemies, real or imaginary. When Americans debate the ABM or SALT talks, when they discuss MIRVs or ICBMs, they assume their government knows how to make and handle nuclear weapons. They are like Corvair owners who thought General Motors knew how to make rear engine compacts. The truth is that the quality of the average nuclear bomb is controlled little better than the quality of the average mass-produced automobile. Defects in production have caused accidental detonations, duds and recall campaigns where nuclear weapons are brought back to the factory for repairs much the same way Fords are called in to repair defective steering assemblies.

The nuclear weapons makers have spent over 17.1 billion dollars supposedly to make America safe for democracy. They have also sunk one South Pacific island and forced the evacuation of two others. They have raised the nation's infant mortality rate, permanently contaminated 250 square miles in Nevada, taken uranium miners to an early grave, contaminated thyroids in Utah and the Marshall Islands, probably hiked the cancer rate in Denver, scattered radioactive debris in Greenland and Spain, triggered small earthquakes in Las Vegas, and polluted the prime Western watershed with radioactive waste.

Safety seems to diminish as the weapons program grows. As the experts gain more experience building nuclear weapons their mistakes get worse. Sixteen years of practice fighting over 200 fires did not teach the men at Colorado's Rocky Flats plutonium fabrication plant how to avert a 45-million-dollar fire in May 1969. Nineteen years experience testing nuclear weapons did not prevent a venting in December 1970 that contaminated work camps and forced evacuation of a major portion of the Nevada Test Site. Detailed medical reports in the 1930s on cancer dangers to uranium miners did not protect the lungs of men who dug this ore in the 1950s and 1960s.

Why has this ongoing tragedy largely escaped the watchful eye of Americans increasingly sensitized to public health and environmental hazards? Why do ecology-minded college students spend more time fighting for biodegradable toilet paper than elimination of this nuclear juggernaut? Why do liberal-minded senators and congressmen lash out against the inhumanity of napalm and then routinely approve billion-dollar appropriations for these infinitely more dangerous hydrogen bombs and warheads? Why does the President pledge millions for cancer research but stand idly by while the nuclear weapons program hikes the cancer rate?

One reason is that Americans prefer to worry about issues close to their daily lives, such as car bumpers that can take five-mile-an-hour impact, nonphosphate detergents, lead-free gasolines, preservation of the redwoods, salvation of the Everglades, or recycling newspapers. The weapons program seems remote to most Americans, even if it is the greatest single threat to the future of the nation and perhaps the world.

The institutionalization of the weapons program also puts the armsmakers beyond all public control or accountability. The first American nuclear bomb was dropped before the nation at large knew there was a nuclear weapons program. In this spirit of secrecy the armsmakers have continued to hide, classify, distort, manipulate and lie until the public has been brainwashed into believing the nuclear weapons program is the foundation of American military defense. Any attack on the weapons program is construed as an attack on national security. Any nuclear arms accident is justified on national security grounds. The care and feeding of an estimated 40,000 nuclear weapons around the globe takes precedence over public health. While claiming to protect us from nuclear attack these scientists are contaminating us with nuclear poisons.

The critics, and there have been many, insist this nuclear armory should be dismantled. Their traditional argument holds that nuclear war is unwinnable and therefore unthinkable. The government seems to agree in principle and says it would disarm tomorrow if it could only persuade the enemy to do likewise. The critics then wring their hands and suggest new proposals for the disarmament negotiating table that might be able to expedite some sort of treaty.

While the disarmament negotiators drone on about counter-force capability, penetration aids, damage denial, X-ray kills and soft facilities, the nuclear armsmakers continue to poison the air, land and soil with increasing quantities of toxic radionuclides. Unilateral nuclear disarmament is in order because our current system of producing, testing, and deploying nuclear weapons is suicidal. A nation unable to manage its own nuclear weapons should condemn them. This book is an account of the mismanagment of the American nuclear weapons program that threatens all our lives.

Doubtless there are those who will interpret such a plea as capitulation to the would-be enemy. They will raise fears of nuclear blackmail and enemy invasion. But we are already being blackmailed by our own nuclear scientists who demand we accept dangerous radiation exposure so we can protect ourselves. We are already being attacked by these nuclear experts who claim they are just testing. The simple truth is that the owner of the nuclear weapons incurs the worst liability. He must accept the nuclear pollution engendered by making, testing and deploying atomic weapons. He must surround his major cities with dangerous plants. He must worry about armed nuclear bombers crashing in his native land. He must also accept the worries of sabotage and the risk that an enemy might humble us by blowing up one of the nuclear stockpiles near all our major cities with conventional weapons. That is one of the many fringe benefits of having nuclear weapons in our own backyard.

Trace the evolution of the great American bomb machine and you see that the armsmakers have been exploiting a nuclear psychosis for three decades. Early in 1939 word passed from Europe that the Germans were working on a uranium project presumably oriented toward an atomic bomb. Leo Szilard and a group of other nuclear scientists who had recently emigrated from Germany to the United States decided that their adopted country must begin work on an atomic bomb of its own, lest the nation be easy prey to the Third Reich. So in July 1939 they persuaded Albert Einstein to sign a letter to President Roosevelt that suggested acceleration of American atomic research, with funding from the Army and Navy. In 1940 the work was expanded by the National Defense Research Council and the following year it was placed under the Office of Science and Research and Development. As technical processes evolved to make uranium and plutonium bombs, the War Department set up the Manhattan Engineering District to develop the necessary manufacturing complex. By the end of the war more than 600,000 Americans had worked on production of four bombs. One was dropped on New Mexico, two were dropped on Japan and the fourth became the first member of our nuclear stockpile. The bill for the four Manhattan Project bombs was 2 billion dollars.

Ironically the German scientists associated with their nation's uranium project never came close to building an atomic bomb. For one thing Hitler had driven many of his best physicists into exile, severely limiting the expertise of his team. The scientists who were left worked with a fair degree of independence. Unlike the American nuclear experts, they were not directly under the thumb of military leadership. While their generals were perpetrating the worst atrocities in human history, these nuclear scientists held serious moral reservations about building an atomic bomb and putting it into the hands of Hitler. They actually convinced Hitler that nuclear energy would be more useful as a power source than a weapon. They used their wartime largesse to facilitate pure research under the facetious slogan: "The war in the cause of German science."

In America precisely the opposite was true and some scientists lived to regret it. One was Leo Szilard who had been instrumental in accelerating nuclear research in 1939. Shortly before the end of the war, he led a petition campaign to block use of the nuclear weapons against Japan. Szilard was unsuccessful and after the war was over Albert Einstein would mourn: "If I had known that the Germans would not succeed in constructing the atom bomb, I would never have moved a finger."

The days following the surrender of Japan found the scientists and statesmen all trying to outdo one another with high-sounding platitudes about putting this nuclear genie back into the bottle. The immediate issue was the fate of the Manhattan Project which had a staff of about 50,000 and a monthly budget of about 100 million dollars at V-J Day. The logical solution at the time would probably have been to condemn nuclear weapons as immoral and dispose of the Manhattan Project apparatus. But this was too simpleminded. The statesmen claimed that before the weapons program could be shut down they would have to work out a treaty to prevent anyone else from developing or using nuclear weapons. Of course no one else had nuclear weapons or knew how to make them. But American experts worried that Russia or some other potential enemy might learn how to make these weapons or steal our secrets.

Thus the original paranoia about nuclear weapons that launched the Manhattan Project was now being converted into a bolshevik scare aimed at keeping the weapons program together. The bomb work gradually began slipping out of the hands of conscientous scientists into the hands of subhumans hell-bent on bigger and better weapons for no purpose. The Nazi nuclear peril, though unfounded, at least gave the World War II scientists some rational basis for nuclear weapons research. But after the war there was no good reason to keep making bombs and many of the top experts got out of the weapons program. Some left with the blessings of General Leslie Groves, head of the Manhattan Project because they had now become security risks. "In the main these men had been engaged in the atomic research project before the Army entered the field and had been retained in the belief that from a security standpoint it was safer to keep them than it was to let them go. I also felt it likely that the American people would demand very rigid security clearances in the future and that this was a time when anyone not possessing a perfect pre-MED [Manhattan project] record could leave the project without stigma of any kind and with full recognition well deserved, of having done a top-notch job for our country."

Groves was referring to the very scientists who might have been able to thwart the gung-ho postwar nuclear spirit. He sought well-rounded soldiers that had enjoyed "a successful athletic career, demonstrating a more than average determination and will to win."

Publicly the Pentagon professed its desire to put the Manhattan Project under civilian control. But behind the scenes General Groves tried to withhold classified nuclear information from relevant senatorial committees and sped ahead on new nuclear tests. The military experts were countered by top Presidential science advisers who lobbied for immediate civilian control of the weapons program. Vannevar Bush, who helped guide nuclear research during World War II, said: "I certainly, as a citizen living in this country after the war, want to see rigid Federal control of what is done in this area. I certainly do not wish to think that some group of experimenters might set up a laboratory half a mile from my house and family and experiment on atomic energy carelessly, poison the neighborhood, or possibly blow it up."

While the experts in Washington continued to echo this theme, military leaders wasted little time setting up their first postwar nuclear tests under the direction of General Curtis E. LeMay. This great sideshow called Crossroads was held in the summer of 1946 in the Marshall Islands. About 42,000 observers came to watch the Pentagon contaminate Bikini atoll so badly that it had to be evacuated until 1968. About the same time this accident was going on, Congress was passing the McMahon act which set up an Atomic Energy Commission to make nuclear energy a "forceful influence for world peace."

Establishment of the Atomic Energy Commission, and its congressional watchdog, the Joint Committee on Atomic Energy, ranks as one of the nation's major legislative disasters. In their zeal to put atomic energy under civilian control, the legislators merely totalitarianized nuclear power. The A.E.C. was given cradle-to-grave power over atomic energy. The agency won the right to finance, license, regulate, and police the entire nuclear field. Today other government agencies involved in the sampling or monitoring of radiation pollution are forced to rely on inadequate A.E.C. data, or are themselves funded and controlled by the A.E.C. Consultants for the atomic energy industry who work under A.E.C. research grants crop up time and again as prime congressional witnesses proclaiming radiation is virtually harmless if kept below a so-called "safe-threshold."

From the beginning the A.E.C.'s prime role has been promotion of nuclear power in all forms. Public health considerations have been a decidedly second-rate matter. The five A.E.C. commissioners have always been men who served as apologists for the weapons program. Their selection has often been dictated by expediency. Two of the five original commissioners had no background at all in atomic matters.

The commissioners, who all have equal voting power, appoint a general manager who takes administrative control of the agency. The close relationship of the agency to the Pentagon is reflected by the fact that three of the first five A.E.C. general managers were military men. Also the A.E.C.'s Division of Military Affairs, which inherited the weapons production job from the Manhattan Project, has traditionally been headed by a career military officer. The Pentagon has also kept its hand in the business through establishment of a postwar Armed Forces Special Weapons Project, known today as the Defense Nuclear Agency. Immediately after the war this joint service agency coordinated test activities, managed the nuclear stockpile, and supervised soldier training for nuclear combat. Gradually the A.E.C. began to take over more of the test function, with the Pentagon playing a subordinate role oriented toward calculating the combat effects of nuclear weapons. Today the A.E.C. has full control over production and testing, while stockpile, training, and strategic deployment functions are handled by the Pentagon. Since World War II the A.E.C. has invested about $11.8 billion to fortify the nation's nuclear stockpile. The Pentagon's Defense Nuclear Agency spent another $2.3 billion on its housekeeping functions and the Office of Civil Defense chipped in another billion to help the nation prepare for nuclear war with fallout shelters, survival biscuits and studies of "post-attack" society.

Putting the weapons production program under the A.E.C. has given Congress and the nation the illusion that the weapons work is under safe civilian control. Unfortunately many of the civilians in control have been hawks like Edward Teller who promoted the bolshevik scare to speed development of bigger weapons. These hawks have weeded out doves who tried to block the excesses of the weapons program. For example, in 1949 J. Robert Oppenheimer, father of the A-bomb, headed an A.E.C. general advisory commission that recommended against construction of an H-bomb. Oppenheimer and the commission were overruled. Teller sped ahead on his H-bomb work, and, when the agency set up its Lawrence Radiation Laboratory at Livermore, California, the Hungarian-born scientist was actually given a veto over the programs of the weapons design lab. In 1953 Oppenheimer was brought up before an A.E.C. personnel security board where Teller charged Oppenheimer with failing to promote the H-bomb effort and trying to discourage other scientists from working on the project. For these and other trumped up security violations, Oppenheimer was stripped of his security clearance for life. Today leaders of the A.E.C. weapons policy continue in the Teller tradition. The head of the A.E.C.'s major nuclear design lab at Los Alamos, New Mexico, is Harold Agnew, widely known in nuclear circles as one of the nation's leading hawks. In the fall of 1970 he was asked about the utility of tactical nuclear weapons. He replied: "It is my belief that if people were to prepare the right spectrum of weapons, we might be able to knock out the sort of foolishness we now have in Vietnam, the Middle East, or anyplace else. If you could develop a [nuclear] weapon with very little yield, a few tons, that could hit systems, I think you could stop things."

Egging on the hawks have been opportunists who realized that development of the nuclear complex through military applications would facilitate industrial and commercial spin-offs. Thus the A.E.C. weapons work subsidized uranium mining on the Colorado Plateau, the construction of plutonium reactors in South Carolina, the expansion of nuclear waste disposal sites in places like Idaho and Washington, plus research grants that have paved the way for so-called peaceful applications that further contaminate the earth. It is doubtful that the nuclear power plants, excavation projects, and gas stimulation tests would have made it, or made it as quickly as they did, had the A.E.C. been without the largesse provided by an inflated weapons program.

Supposedly the entire weapons program and the A.E.C. have been under the careful scrutiny of the Joint Committee on Atomic Energy (J.C.A.E.). Unfortunately this committee has abdicated its congressional watchdog function to play trained seal, barking on command to promote the glories of the atomic age. Members include people like Representative Craig Hosmer (Republican of California) who quit his job with the A.E.C. to run for Congress so he could get a seat on the J.C.A.E. When nuclear accidents happen, as they frequently do, Hosmer and his friends on the J.C.A.E. do their best to help the A.E.C. suppress the details or at least defend the mistakes. The J.C.A.E. members are ready to fly anywhere at a moment's notice to champion the agency cause.

These are some of the many reasons why the great American bomb machine has gotten away with murder. The A.E.C. makes the weapons free of virtually all public control. Had the production process remained in Pentagon hands, the public might have gone against the weapons program at an early date. But under its holy civilian aura the A.E.C. has been able to perpetrate continual atrocities. Congressmen responsible for this corrupt agency are off playing nuclear cheerleader. The ecologists are more worried about oil spills than plutonium spills. Statesmen who should be trying to disarm America are off in Helsinki or Vienna trying to disarm Russia. Scientists who have penetrated the myth that nuclear weapons are safe and easy to handle are eased out or forced to quit. And all the while, says former Pentagon research chief Herbert York, "The power to decide whether or not doomsday has arrived is in the process of passing from statesmen and politicians to lower level officers and technicians and eventually to machines."

CHAPTER THREE

PRODUCTION

Brigadier General Edward Giller, who heads the A.E.C.'s 800-million-dollar-a-year Division of Military Application (D.M.A.), insists there is absolutely no place for sloppy control in the nuclear-bomb business. In an April 15, 1970, speech to an American Management Association seminar on "Product Liability and Its Effects on Top Management and Corporate Legal Policies," General Giller said: "I don't believe I need to elaborate on the potential human, political, and dollar costs which could attend an accident leading to a nuclear detonation. There is no comparison with the inconvenience experienced when your car won't start or your electric oven heating element fails."

As chief of American nuclear-weapons production, General Giller explained the problem even better to the House Public Works Subcommittee on October 1, 1970. He was telling why the A.E.C. needed 265 million dollars to rebuild and remodel facilities that "have a potential for major loss through fire or explosion with the attendant consequences of serious disruptions of major programs and possible offsite and onsite exposures of persons to radioactive or other hazardous materials." The money would go for safety improvements at ten facilities in the A.E.C. weapons complex. Eight of them are "plutonium-handling facilities containing radioactivity. They have sufficient material in them during a day's operation, and heat-generating flammables that are part of the process so that if a major fire were to break out and break through the building, that is breach the roof, then hundreds of square miles could be involved in radiation exposure and involve cleanup at an astronomical cost as well as creating a very intense reaction by the general public exposed to this."

Few Americans understand the magnitude of the problem because so little is known about the weapons business. The production process begins when the Pentagon sends the A.E.C. a purchase order for a new-model hydrogen bomb or warhead. Since scientists worked out most nuclear weapons fundamentals during the 1940s and 1950s, research and development work now focuses on shaping the weapon into desired warhead configurations. Experts try to achieve the specified nuclear yield with the smallest possible payload. They must insure the weapon will fire on command yet be foolproof when stockpiled or transported.

Two University of California laboratories at Los Alamos, New Mexico, and Livermore, California, propose competing bomb designs in the same way Boeing and Lockheed bid for an Air Force contract. Dr. Harold Agnew, director of the Los Alamos laboratory, says: "Each outfit comes back and boasts that its golden chariot is smaller, cheaper, and will give more bang for buck. The net result is that we end up saving money for the public and getting the best possible weapon. It works just like free enterprise." General Giller agrees: "Competition between the labs gives you drive within each organization. I believe that having two competing nuclear labs has enabled us to stay ahead of the competition in the state of the art."

After Los Alamos or Livermore wins a bomb bid, the job is fed into the A.E.C.'s production complex. First, the winning lab submits final designs for nuclear components. Then, Sandia Corporation, a subsidiary of American Telephone and Telegraph's Western Electric Company, makes the nonnuclear component designs at its facilities in Livermore or Albuquerque. After extensive laboratory and field testing, the designs are turned over to the

A.E.C. manufacturing complex operated by private contractors. Dow Chemical's Rocky Flats, Colorado, plant fabricates the plutonium components that trigger the nuclear weapons. In Kansas City, Bendix Corporation makes the electro and electromechanical parts. Detonators come from Monsanto Research Corporation in Dayton, Ohio, and the neutron generators are supplied by a General Electric plant in Pinellas, Florida. The finished components are shipped to the Pantex, Texas (near Amarillo), or Burlington, Iowa, final assembly plants run by Mason and Hanger-Silas Mason, Inc.

The assembly teams practice on dummy or "wooden" bombs before starting on a new weapons series. General Giller says, "We give them a very thick manual that lists step-by-step procedures for putting together each bomb. It might say, 'Take wrench 3 and make two full turns on bolt A, then take off nut 7 with wrench 8.' Everything is done by checklist, right down to the length of time allowed for letting the paint dry. We are very careful. I hope the Russians are, too."

After a new weapons series is checked out at the Nevada test site, the bombs are shipped by air, rail and truck to American military commands at home and abroad. Periodically the weapons are spot-checked for defects. When several weapons in the same series show up with similar defects, then the whole series is recalled. General Giller says: "It's pretty much like the auto industry. When they find the right front end falling off certain police cars, they bring them all back in for a fix. When we find high explosives deteriorating in, say, our Model-T bomb series, then we will bring them all back to the factory for a look. Nuclear components are usually repaired at Rocky Flats, nonnuclear components are handled at Pantex or Burlington. Of course, sometimes the boys in the field can do the repairs themselves. We just send a fix kit to each affected stockpile site and instruct them on how to do the repairs. Sometimes they might just dab on a bit of glue, or change an electrical connection. Simple stuff.

"The A.E.C. got into this program accidentally. Back in the late 1950s someone noticed deterioration in some of the stockpile weapons. A broad check turned up more problems. So we decided to initiate the comprehensive stockpile surveillance program. We spot-check certain weapons in each series and even pull some out of the stockpile for a trip to Nevada, where they are detonated in underground reliability tests. We have to make sure the older weapons still fire when they are supposed to and don't fire when they're not supposed to. I sure hope the Russians do the same thing."

As the weapons become outmoded, they are reclaimed from the operational military commands. Some are shipped to the Air Force's "dead storage" site in Manzano Mountain, just outside of Albuquerque. This is probably the largest nuclear-weapons stockpile site in the world. The vintage bombs are put to rest in caves behind steel doors. Others weapons are taken back to Pantex or Burlington, where they are dismantled. Long before recycling became an ecological fad, men at these two plants were conserving nuclear-bomb components. All the plutonium is carefully removed and shipped back to Rocky Flats, where it is fabricated for new weapons. General Giller believes even "the plutonium in that one bomb left over from World War II is part of another bomb today. We don't waste anything."

The Burlington and Pantex plants are among those General Giller would like to remodel. Like much of the weapons complex, these units are World War II vintage and need about 33.5 million dollars' worth of improvements, including new fire walls, ventilators, and added protection for weapons production bays. Both were originally Army ordnance plants designed for making conventional explosives, not nuclear weapons. Accidents in the various weapons-production units are not infrequent; in fact, this is why different bomb components are isolated in separate storage vaults known as "igloos." General Giller says, "We keep the components apart so that an explosion in one igloo doesn't blow up another. The main idea is to prevent blowing ourselves up, or at least only blowing up one part of ourselves at a time." This is no small problem. On November 13, 1963, three employees at the A.E.C.'s Medina works in San Antonio were busy dismantling the high-explosive component of a nuclear bomb when something went wrong. The bomb was being retired from the nuclear-weapons stockpile and the high explosive was supposed to be taken to a disposal site where it could be safely burned. Unfortunately the explosive began burning spontaneously. The fire quickly spread to similar components in other bombs. After a small explosion took place, the three men retreated to safety just before 120,000 tons of explosive ignited and sent up a cloud of uranium and other bomb debris. The A.E.C. marveled that the explosion caused only "light property damage" to nearby homes and insisted that the scattered uranium was not a health hazard to the populace. But the people in San Antonio were not particularly dismayed when the weapons work at Medina was phased out in 1966 and consolidated with production activities in Pantex and Burlington.

The Burlington plant has had some problems, particularly with remote-controlled presses that form chemical high explosives into shape for the bomb. On February 24, 1964, a high explosive detonated during processing and caused some 60,000 dollars' worth of damage. A similar accident on June 2, 1967, caused 50,000 dollars' damage.

Even insufficient weatherproofing has hurt the weapons production complex. On the afternoon of September 3, 1967, two storms merged over Borger, Texas, and swept south across Carson County toward the Pantex plant. By the time the storm reached Pantex, the winds were gusting to 100 miles an hour and hailstones were as big as oranges. It moved across the security fence and skidded over ordnance storage magazines. The storm appeared headed southwest and away from the heart of the facility, when suddenly it veered straight into the administrative, manufacturing, assembly and warehouse sections of the plant, before moving southward and eventually dying out.

That night A.E.C. officials cut short their Labor Day weekend to rush back and examine what the storm had done to America's main H-bomb assembly plant. They found their facility, supposedly hardened against enemy attack, had been humbled by a simple hailstorm. The roof of the administration building was partially ripped off and executive offices were under water. The cyclone security fence was down at several points so guards were posted to keep sightseers out. Walls, doors, roofs and ramps in weapons-assembly buildings, warehouses, garages and sheds were smashed. Ninety-two of 120 plant vehicles and several trailers were overturned. There was also damage to the electrical-power distribution system, steam-condensate return and compressed-air distribution system. Employees were given a week's extension on their Labor Day holiday while repair crews cleaned up the debris, totaling 1.7 million dollars in damages.

Four years after the Pantex devastation pertinent facts on the damage were highly classified. The agency conceded that nuclear-weapons components were damaged in the storm but refused to divulge the details.

Strict security shrouds the entire weapons-production process. The A.E.C. spent about 7.89 million dollars on security investigations of 17,300 prospective employees in fiscal 1970. This special "Q Clearance" investigation takes months. One investigator even talked to a prospective employee's first-grade teacher, who was eighty-four years old.

Visitors to all A.E.C. weapons facilities must wear badges and be accompanied by escorts, even when they go to the bathroom. The official rationale for all this secrecy is national security. A.E.C. public-relations officers ask writers "not to give any of our secrets away to the Russians." At a time when six nations have atom bombs and most high-school physics students know the basics of atom-bomb making, this is nonsense. The real reason for this security is to keep the A.E.C.'s secrets from the Americans. These secrets are not the physics of nuclear demolition but the chemistry of nuclear pollution. Proof is provided by the A.E.C.'s model operation, Rocky Flats. The agency says this plant "ranks first in A.E.C. facilities for safety and holds the fourth best all-time mark in American industry—2,122 consecutive days (24,-295,524 man hours) without a disabling injury."

If Rocky Flats is the safest plant in the A.E.C., one hates to think about what is going on at the agency's other weapons plants. Since the plutonium-fabrication facility opened in 1953, there have been more than 200 fires. During one 16-month period there were 24 fires, explosions, plutonium spills and contamination incidents at the plant. The fires and secret burial of radioactive waste

have contaminated Denver's water and soil and will probably increase the local cancer rate, according to biomedical experts at the
Lawrence Radiation Laboratory, Livermore, California. Rocky
Flats scientists have written that at least 325 workmen have been
contaminated by radiation over the years. The plant physician reports that 56 out of 7,400 workers got cancer during the first 17
years of operation; 14 subsequently died. The plant manager says
this cancer rate is "meager," but refuses to conduct a full epidemiological study that would verify his contention.

One might reasonably ask how the A.E.C.'s safest plant
could produce its worst accident. The answer begins with ground-
breaking back in 1951. Siting the nation's largest plutonium processing facility 16 miles upwind of downtown Denver was a tragic,
perhaps fatal error. This grayish metal, worth 43 dollars a gram,
is one of the most dangerous substances known. Minute quantities
inhaled or imbedded in the skin can be lethal. It has a radioactive
half-life of 24,400 years. Plutonium's radiation will damage living
cells, leading to bone and lung cancer. Because it oxidizes quickly,
plutonium is a serious fire threat. Even during World War II,
Manhattan Project leaders knew better than to put a major plutonium works near an urban area. Lieutenant General Leslie R.
Groves, the head of the Manhattan Project, rejected siting a new
plutonium facility near Oak Ridge, Tennessee, because he "felt
uneasy about the danger to the surrounding population. Oak
Ridge was not far from Knoxville. . . . If . . . a reactor were to
explode and throw great quantities of highly radioactive materials
into the atmosphere when the wind was blowing toward Knoxville,
the loss of life and the damage to health in the area might be cata-
strophic." The scientists finally agreed on guidelines for siting the
plutonium pile and separation plant. First, the entire complex
should be surrounded by a rectangular hazardous-manufacturing
area approximately 12 by 16 miles. The pile and separation plant
should be at least eight miles from the laboratory, ten miles downwind from the employees' village, 20 miles from any town over
1,000 and 20 miles from the nearest highway or railroad plant.
These criteria finally led to siting the plutonium works on a half
million acres of arid land at remote Hanford, Washington. An

eight-lane road was built to the Hanford works because Groves wanted to have extra lanes available for evacuation in the event of an accident.

But all these criteria for siting the Hanford Plutonium Works were abandoned in 1951, when Rocky Flats was selected over six other sites. The cow pasture at the front range of the Colorado Rockies was not a safe location, but did offer other compensations. It was close to the Denver labor pool, the University of Colorado, adequate utilities and transportation. Promising scientists gladly transferred to "Rocky," where they could ski, hunt and fish in the nearby mountains on days off. The plant grew quickly. Architecture was utilitarian, giving the appearance of a trailer park inside an oil refinery.

On the inside workmen set up elaborate plutonium-fabrication lines. Long rows of ventilated, shielded stainless-steel glove boxes were installed and connected by conveyors. Each box was fitted with portholes and sealed with rubber gloves that permitted the workmen to handle the plutonium without contamination. Pieces of plutonium were fed into the production line where workmen would form, press, mill, machine, polish or calibrate the metal at their respective glove boxes. To guard against accidentally releasing plutonium into the atmosphere, the entire production area was sealed off in a self-contained structure with an internal filtration system. An elaborate network of automatic heat and radiation sensors and roving teams of safety monitors were put to work guarding against accidents.

As fabrication of pyrophoric plutonium grew, so did fires. The worst of the early blazes came on September 11, 1957, when a small amount of plutonium ignited spontaneously inside a glove box in the supposedly "fireproof" final production area. Firefighters were so used to this kind of plutonium fire in the ventilated, enclosed glove-box production lines that they reacted slowly. They feared a quick response might spread the toxic radioactive fumes or create a nuclear explosion. Finally they decided to switch ventilating fans on to high speed. But this backfired and sent flames racing through the production lines igniting more plutonium. The fire burned flammable radiation filters that were designed to prevent radiation from escaping the glove boxes and the building. Water also damaged the filters and plutonium contaminated the Denver area. An attempt to extinguish the fire with carbon dioxide failed, so water was used, and 13 hours later the flames were finally out. The small fire caused 818,600 dollars' damage.

Even the A.E.C.'s Division of Operational Safety was appalled: "It appears [by hindsight] irrational that facilities were ever designed . . . to permit hazards from a relatively insignificant amount of material to influence so strongly the chain of events which led to a major loss."

Rocky Flats officials saved face from this disaster by going out after an A.E.C. safety award. Just six days after the fire, while recovery teams were sifting through the ruins, Rocky Flats embarked on its marathon safety dance, 2,122 consecutive days without a disabling accident. This record, which still ranks first in the A.E.C., was compiled under the dubious assumption that the only accident is one where the worker has "lost time" from his job. Time lost due to cancer does not count, because plant officials claim it is virtually impossible to get cancer from Rocky Flats plutonium.

During the first 13 months of this record-breaking safety period there were 21 fires, explosions, radioactive material spills and contamination incidents inside the plant. Union officials were particularly upset about management's reluctance to bring in health physicists (who monitor worker health) for radiation monitoring after serious accidents occurred. At A.E.C. radiation hazard hearings in Washington during March 1959 they raised serious doubts about the safety of the plant. The union men testified that on October 28, 1959, a "chip fire in a production area occurred and as usual health physicists were notified. No air samples were taken nor were any respirators worn to guard against inhaling dangerous plutonium. Health physicists learned of this operation after a worker involved in it coughed up black sputum at his home and became . . . concerned with the method in which the incident had been handled by his superiors."

The union leaders also pointed out that on October 28, 1958, supervisory personnel instructed workers to clean up a radioactive-materials spill "using no respirators and without health physicists being informed of the situation." Subsequently health physicists were notified and recommended respirators and "area supervision cleanup operations of the spill."

On October 3, 1958, another supervisor "stopped health physicists from allowing men to know what the airborne contamination was in their production area on the grounds that it was his business only as to what the level was."

A variety of serious contamination incidents was reported in supposedly "cold" (nonradioactive) areas. For example, on September 10, 1958, a "cafeteria survey showed 50 to 54 smears [taken to measure radiation] to be over allowable tolerance level." On October 9, 1958, 97 of 99 smears in the locker room also showed contamination. Radioactivity was also found on drinking fountains, sinks, laundered caps, shoes, drums, flasks, carts, lifts and saws in cold areas.

Accidents like these continued right up to the end of the momentous 2,122-day safety period. On June 20, 1963, less than one month before Rocky Flats received its first-place plaque, a leak developed in an overhead line transferring a plutonium solution between laboratories. The radioactive solution dripped through a false ceiling, over walls and onto the floor. Decontamination cost 8,364 dollars.

By the end of Rocky Flats' first decade, plant scientists had gathered sufficient data on worker contamination to publish important articles in the sober international journal *Health Physics*. In 1964 two experts wrote about "the Rocky Flats wound counter, which was developed in 1957 to measure the amount of plutonium contamination present in wounds incurred in process areas. Since that time more than 900 wounds have been monitored of which more than 300 have indicated some degree of plutonium contamination. However, in cases where the plutonium is deeply imbedded or where physical impairment might result from complete excision, small amounts of plutonium may be left in the wound."

In 1965 union officials decided to make a strong pitch for a new safety package in their contract negotiations with Dow. They asked for a joint "Radiation Safety Committee" with the company that would meet bimonthly "to discuss problems arising from radiation safety complaints from any employees." They also proposed adding three union members to the company's Executive Safety Council and making radiation records of all employees available to the "union at least once a year in writing."

At the same time management was blocking all these proposals in the front office, more workers were being contaminated in the production area. On March 19, 1965, a glove-box failure resulted in plutonium contamination of one man's lung. Six days later an employee's left shoulder was contaminated with an acidified plutonium nitrate solution. Activation of a new transfer line on May 6 sprayed an acid solution out of a loose joint. Decontamination cost 7,557 dollars. On October 15, 1965, a 17,000-dollar fire contaminated workers throughout the production area. Then on November 9, 1965, a 23,253-dollar explosion and fire contaminated 12 more workers. All of these accidents occurred during another "no-injury" period when Rocky Flats claimed to be building up 11,802,581 man-hours without a disabling accident.

By 1967 *Health Physics* readers could see the Rocky Flats situation was getting worse. Plant experts reported that the October 15, 1965, fire had contaminated 25 workers with up to 17 times the maximum permissible plutonium exposure. In another article that year three Rocky Flats scientists described the gradual amputation of the thumb and second finger of a worker injured by the explosive reaction between hot plutonium metal and carbon tetrachloride. Eleven months after the amputation "it was thought that there was a high concentration of plutonium in a small portion of the remaining thumb stump." But the operation was only a partial success and six months later "the remaining portion of thumb was removed."

Plant security, vigorously enforced by the F.B.I., suppressed the details of the growing crisis inside the plant. At monthly "safety meetings" workers were threatened with loss of their security clearances, and jobs, plus possible prosecution for divulging classified information. A former F.B.I. agent named Mike Carroll handled Dow public relations, keeping information about accidents as quiet as possible. Finally, in the fall of 1967, a few members of Rocky Flats Local 15440 of the International Union of District 50 leaked the magic word: cancer. At the time the coal-conscious international leadership of the United Mine Workers was conducting a vigorous campaign against a proposed nuclear power plant at Platteville, 30 miles north of Denver. Spearheading the campaign was the Ralph Nader of the atomic-energy industry, Washington atomic-energy consultant, Leo Goodman.

Goodman, who was then atomic-energy advisor to the United Auto Workers, joined U.M.W. leaders in a trip to Denver, where they worked to block the proposed atomic power plant at Platteville. After reading in a Denver paper that Goodman was in town, a group of Rocky Flats employees visited him at his motel room. They told the atomic-hazards expert that plant safety was falling apart. They reviewed case histories of workers who had contracted cancer and then been denied medical pensions. Reporters for the *United Mine Workers Journal* and *Cervi's Journal,* a muckraking Denver business weekly, were present and published accounts of the meeting. To the chagrin of Dow officials and leaders of Rocky Flats Local 15440 of District 50 of the U.M.W., the stories pointed out that "officials of District 50 of the U.M.W. representing the Dow Chemical workers will not discuss the radiation dangers involved for workers at Rocky Flats. If they do, they face loss of their security clearance."

This story ignited a feud within the U.M.W. International leaders of the U.M.W. were already sore at District 50 (with a regional office in Denver) because it refused to join their fight against the proposed atomic plant in Platteville. After the stories on the meeting with Goodman were published, District 50 officials went out of their way to back the new atomic plant. In February 1968 a delegation of Rocky Flats local 15440 leaders headed by President Jim Kelly traveled to Washington for a regional directors conference of District 50. Aided by their Denver regional director, Sam Franklin, the Rocky Flats union leaders extolled the virtues of the safety program at their plant. Using color slides provided by the Rocky Flats management, they showed how "the Rocky Flats plant has achieved one of the world's best safety records . . . through a highly effective program of industrial safety."

They pointed out that "the design of Rocky Flats facilities insures that each worker's exposure to radiation is kept to a minimum. . . . The average work-related exposure of a Rocky Flats employee for an entire year is barely above the radiation received during a chest X ray." Gene DeCarlo, chairman of the union's radiation committee, told how "all employees are particularly careful about cuts and scratches on their flesh as the radiation danger increases in an open flesh." The assembled directors were so impressed by the presentation that they subsequently passed a resolution calling for the expansion of District 50's role in the atomic-power industry.

Back at Rocky Flats, workers soon received news of the meeting in the February 26, 1968, edition of District 50 *News*. The lead story reported that District 50 International President Elwood Moffett had declared that his union's future was clearly interwoven with the progress and development of the atomic-energy industry. Further, the International Executive Board of District 50 had promised to "continue to represent and safeguard our membership employed in every phase of that industry."

The paper also carried the text of District 50's resolution endorsing atomic power plants, "contrary to the thinking of those who sporadically would remind us that progress in the field of nuclear energy represents a destructive force which could annihilate humanity, mounting scientific statistics amassed through the 2,000 manyears of experience in the atomic industry discount this pessimism."

Representative Chet Holifield, chairman of the Joint Committee on Atomic Energy, inserted the District 50 resolution into the *Congressional Record*. Beneath a story on Holifield's action in the March 11, 1968, *News* issue was a filler that did not amuse the Rocky Flats workers: "1.4 million Americans now alive have been cured of cancer. Early detection and prompt treatment saved their lives. The American Cancer Society urges you to become familiar with cancer's seven warning signals and to fight the disease with a checkup and a check."

The international leadership of the United Mine Workers was also not amused by District 50's endorsement of atomic power at the expense of coal. In March 1968 the U.M.W. International expelled District 50, charging that it was "willing to risk the lives of every citizen of this country in potential nuclear-reactors accidents for the sake of a few members they have in atomic plants."

After the break, District 50 began getting along better with Dow and worse with the U.M.W. In March 1968, just after District 50 endorsed atomic power, one of its biggest locals, 12075 in Midland, Michigan, set a "chemical industry precedent" by winning an 80-cent-plus, three-year package from Dow. This paved the way for a 60-cent-an-hour direct wage hike plus a wage reopener in the third year for Rocky Flats Local 15440. The union ratified this package in June 1968. Unfortunately, 15440 again lost its demand for the safety package originally proposed in 1965.

The U.M.W., through Leo Goodman, subsequently charged that "because the workers revealed the real hazards in the *U.M.W. Journal* and *Cervi's Journal* of Denver [in November 1967] . . . a sweetheart agreement was negotiated between District 50, Dow and the A.E.C. [June 1968] to foreclose any public discussion of the unsafe operating practices in the Rocky Flats plant. . . . Thus, in order to cozy up to Dow Chemical, District 50 not only abandoned labor's traditional role in behalf of workers' safety in the plant, but also collaborated with A.E.C.-Dow Chemical in hiding from the people of the Denver community the great hazard which this plant brought to them."

Rocky Flats Local 15440 President Jim Kelly denied this. The senior radiation monitor said: "If anyone told me to my face that we were playing sweetheart with management, I'd knock him clear across the table. The real problem is that individual workers are afraid to turn their own plant health records (which they are eligible to see) over to the union. They think they'll lose their job. . . . These guys raise a lot of hell in the locker room, but they don't have the courage to get involved."

The bickering continued as the safety situation deteriorated further. Perhaps the worst accident of 1968 came when a quantity of oil contaminated with plutonium was scooped up, placed in a drum and trucked off for disposal at official A.E.C. burial grounds in Idaho. En route across the plant ground, however, the drum began to leak. Over a mile of highway was contaminated. The A.E.C.'s solution was to repave the road. Unfortunately plutonium's half-life of 24,400 years is a good deal longer than the full-life of asphalt, and years from now, when the roadbed wears away, the hot plutonium will be exposed, to contaminate unborn generations.

By the spring of 1969 small fires were breaking out in the production area at a rate of one a month. Fortunately the fire department was able to extinguish them in time. But on Sunday May 11, 1969, plutonium stored in a cabinet ignited spontaneously and flames jumped into the maze of glove boxes. Heat detectors that should have sensed the blaze immediately, didn't. Guards who should have been monitoring the 776-777 building were not there. By the time the fire alarm sounded at 2:27 P.M., the blaze was out of control.

When company firemen reached 776-777 they found tons of flammable radiation shielding feeding the blaze. The firefighters donned respirators and charged into the dense smoke. Standard procedure ruled out use of water on plutonium fires for fear it might create a nuclear explosion. But the firemen began running out of carbon dioxide within ten minutes and started spraying water on the flames. The men worked in shifts; at times the smoke billowed so thickly they were forced to crawl out along exit lines painted on the floor. By 6:40 P.M. the fire was under control, though it continued to burn in isolated areas through the night.

The first reported damage estimate on the May 11 fire was three million dollars. Days later masked survey teams finally made their way through the radioactive debris and counted up 45 million dollars' damage. It had been the worst industrial fire in American history. Hundreds of Rocky Flats regulars and summertime college employees would spend the better part of two years recovering 20 million dollars' worth of plutonium burned in the fire. To get it they would have to scrub walls, ceilings, floors and production equipment. When cleanup crew morale sagged, the Dow management piped in Muzak to recover plutonium by. One sixty-two-year-old janitor feared plutonium contamination and refused to join the cleanup. He was fired.

Potentially the disaster was the biggest step the United States has ever taken toward nuclear disarmament. The 20 million dollars' worth of plutonium consumed in the fire was sufficient to build 77 atom bombs like the one that incinerated Nagasaki. But rather than signal Geneva or Vienna, Congress quickly shelled out 45 million dollars in supplemental funds to clear up the disaster, a figure equal to the entire fiscal 1969 Rocky Flats budget. And while cleanup crews rehabilitated 776-777, construction crews moved ahead on a 75-million-dollar expansion program that would increase Rocky Flats capacity by 50 percent.

The accident and the expansion program particularly irritated a group of scientists from local universities and industries who had recently formed the Colorado Committee for Environmental Information. They went to Rocky Flats and asked Dow-A.E.C. to monitor Denver area soil for possible plutonium contamination from the fire. In August 1969, Dow-A.E.C. refused to make the plutonium soil tests. They told the C.C.E.I. that technical difficulties would make such a study inconclusive. So in the fall C.C.E.I.'s Dr. Edward Martell, a nuclear chemist with the National Center for Atmospheric Research, began conducting his own soil tests for plutonium in his spare time. Dr. Martell, a West Point graduate, nuclear chemist and former Pentagon specialist in nuclear-weapons testing, concluded his work in December. The result: highly lethal plutonium particles had definitely escaped from Rocky Flats into metropolitan Denver. The worst contamination was in areas east and southeast of the plant toward the Denver suburbs of Broomfield, Westminster and Arvada. High levels of plutonium were also found in Great Western Reservoir, part of the Broomfield water supply. The contamination of Denver ranged from ten to 200 times higher than plutonium fallout deposited by all atomic-bomb testing. And it was nearly 100 times higher than the amount plant spokesmen said was being emitted.

The A.E.C. and Dow sprang into action to try to blunt Martell's facts. The counteroffensive began in early December, when General Giller learned of Martell's independent study and ordered the Rocky Flats staff to initiate similar work. Stanley Hammond, a chemist at Rocky Flats, even contacted Martell and asked for technical advice on how to make good soil tests for plutonium. Martell not only told him how to do it but sent some of his own soil samples over to Rocky Flats. The A.E.C. study essentially corroborated Martell's data. General Giller said, "We find his results are accurate, we don't disagree with his new data. As far as measurements, sampling techniques, and knowledge of science we think Martell is a very competent scientist. Of course, we question his interpretation of his data. While it is true that some plutonium is escaping from the plant, we don't believe it presents a significant health hazard to Denver." The A.E.C. elaborated on this point in February 1970 after release of Martell's report angered Coloradans: "Rocky Flats has released trace amounts of plutonium. . . . However, these quantities have never shown a level of radioactivity in excess of the natural background radiation."

"Background radiation" is a favorite A.E.C. ploy. Because the plutonium oxide particles from Rocky Flats emit dangerous alpha radiation, the agency tries to compare them with naturally occurring (background) particles that also emit alpha radiation. Dr. Arthur R. Tamplin, an A.E.C. expert on the physiological effects of radiation who has become increasingly critical of his employer, explains what all this means for Denver: "The Martell study shows about one trillion pure plutonium oxide particles [plutonium oxidizes in fire] have escaped from Rocky Flats. These are very hot particles. You may only have to inhale 300 of them to double your risk of lung cancer. Inhaled plutonium oxide produces very intense alpha radiation dosage to lung tissue, thousands of times higher than the intensity for radioactive fallout particles and millions of times more intense than the dose from natural alpha radioactivity. An inhaled plutonium oxide particle stays in your lungs for an average of two years, emitting radiation that can destroy lung tissue. If the Rocky Flats plutonium is being redistributed as Martell suggests, then it could increase the lung cancer rate for Denver by as much as ten percent. This could lead to as many as 2,000 additional lung cancers in Denver."

Martell based his initial report on about 90 soil samples but believes thousands more are necessary for full insight into the extent of contamination. He urged the federal government, independent of the A.E.C., to launch a comprehensive soil-testing program in the Denver area.

Both federal and state agencies heeded Martell's call for a review of Rocky Flats, but their studies were neither comprehensive nor independent. During the spring and summer of 1970, President Nixon's top scientific advisory group, the Office of Science and Technology (O.S.T.), conducted an "independent analysis through the A.E.C.'s New York–based Health and Safety Laboratory (H.A.S.L.)." Two H.A.S.L. scientists went to Denver and took 33 soil samples with the help of two Rocky Flats employees. A second independent study of Rocky Flats contamination was conducted by the Colorado State Department of Health. The agency collected soil samples at 325 locations around Denver and sent them to the Environmental Protection Agency's (formerly U. S. Public Health Service) Southwestern Radiological Health Laboratory for analysis. The Las Vegas–based laboratory's primary job is monitoring the A.E.C.'s Nevada test site, paid for by the A.E.C.

Neither Martell nor the C.C.E.I. was surprised when both "independent" federal and state studies concluded Rocky Flats wasn't a threat to Denver. Martell's response was to continue soil testing on his own time with funds out of his research budget at the National Center for Atmospheric Research. As he studied more samples, Martell realized he was finding plutonium that had been deposited before the May 1969 fire. It must have escaped through some other accident. But which accident?

At first, Martell theorized that all this plutonium had escaped during the 1957 fire or perhaps it was the result of a chronic low-level stack effluent. But there was so much. How did it seep through the ground into Old Woman's Creek and the Great Western Reservoir? Was it possible that some of the wastes had been secretly and illicitly buried?

This seemed dubious inasmuch as A.E.C. regulations stipulate that all radioactive waste must be enshrined in special dumps. For example, after the 1969 fire, 330,000 cubic feet of radioactive wastes were shipped to the A.E.C. burial grounds in Idaho by rail car. There can be no compromise with the public safety here; unlicensed burial or storage of radioactive waste could easily contaminate ground and water, particularly in an area like Denver.

But, to the surprise of Martell, the Joint Committee on Atomic Energy and most of the workers at Rocky Flats, radioactive waste had indeed been buried on the plant site. During the 1950s some 1,405 drums of contaminated waste were buried inside and outside the plant gate. The details were made public in a statement on July 21, 1970. Rocky Flats General Manager Lloyd Joshel said that "in view of the increased interest in environmental matters, we decided to remove any concern by reclaiming the waste material from the main burial site. This has been completed. . . . The remaining burials are still being evaluated by Dow with the A.E.C. but the radiation levels are so low that I am personally recommending no further retrieval be made."

Much of the "increased interest in environmental matters" at Rocky Flats was generated by an April 10, 1970, meeting in Washington at the offices of the Joint Committee on Atomic Energy. It was here that James Kelly, president of Rocky Flats Local 15440, first told government atomic-energy officials about the unlicensed burials. The union made the revelation in an effort to get the A.E.C to pressure Dow to accept its old "safety committee" idea, which was being resurrected during contract negotiations.

Present at the meeting were the J.C.A.E.'s ranking majority and minority members, Chet Holifield (Democrat of California) and Craig Hosmer (Republican of California). Their love for anything atomic overcomes any partisam differences between them and has led atomic-energy insiders to dub them "Tweedledee and Tweedledum." Among others who took an active role in the meeting were A.E.C. General Manager Robert Hollingsworth, Assistant General Manager for Operations John A. Erlewine, and J.C.A.E. staff member Captain Edward J. Bauser.

The J.C.A.E.'s own edited transcript of the discussion shows that Kelly began by pointing out that the union had actively supported Dow and the A.E.C. in the face of Martell's criticism. Local 15440 had issued a statement to the press saying, "All the employees would not work there or keep families near if they thought conditions at Rocky Flats were dangerous."

J.C.A.E. Chairman Holifield expressed his deep appreciation for this vote of confidence: "I think most of us feel you have been cooperative and that you [the union leaders] have been placed on the defensive by . . . people like Leo Goodman . . . as well as these professors [Dr. Martell] who have been scratching around in the sand trying to find something wrong within the radius of 50 miles."

KELLY: We don't want to fight. We don't want to start a reaction out there in which the press or anyone else starts getting involved. We have done our part. We have done much better than the company has.

HOLLINGSWORTH: I think the A.E.C. should say here that the attitude of overall support that the union has given to the general environmental question has helped tremendously in terms of our general acceptance by the local area out there. This has been most important. I think we ought to recognize that and we do recognize it.

MCILVENY [*another union leader*]: That is the reason we are splitting from the United Mine Workers.

HOLLINGSWORTH: We appreciate it. That help is very meaningful to our whole problem.

HOLIFIELD [after further discussion on the union safety proposal]: I would like to understand what this burial ground and stream pollution problem is. Will you please tell us? This is something new to me.

KELLY: The company told us a week or so ago, Mr. Chairman, that it was determined some ten or 15 years ago to place some 55-gallon drums of hot waste, oils, and what have you in trenches inside the perimeter of the plant and cover it with dirt, I didn't know this, and I guess a lot of people didn't know it. They haven't put anything in there since 1965 and I don't know who ordered it to be done. We did get these rumors so we took it to the table with the company and with good faith on our part. The minutes of these meetings are published so I began the meeting by asking that those minutes be impounded with the security department and not published and sent out to the stewards and supervisors in order to prevent it from leaking out in the plant until the company had a chance to respond. We still have those minutes impounded.

HOLIFIELD: Let me ask John Erlewine this. Do you know anything about this?

ERLEWINE: I first heard about it in getting ready to come to this meeting.

HOLIFIELD: If your Mr. Abbott [*the A.E.C. area representative*] knew about this situation boiling out there, why didn't he tell you? Why does it have to come to this committee to Bob Hollingsworth and then to you if there is trouble brewing out there? Maybe this is not putting one milligram of radiation above ground, but you know the problems this sort of thing can create from a public relations standpoint. . . .

ERLEWINE: I am not sure I can answer precisely, Mr. Holifield.

BAUSER: Mr. Chairman, I don't think we know right now whether it was an authorized burial or not. It was a very poorly supervised thing.

HOLIFIELD: . . . I understand you don't know whether it is uranium or plutonium. This would be a very serious thing if Dow was taking upon itself the burial of plutonium waste without going through the established procedures. I would assume if this is low-level waste that there would be probably a prohibition against this convenient burial and that it should have been put in some permanent high-level waste burial ground like we have at Hanford.

BAUSER: I don't know but I doubt if that site is an authorized burial site for any level of waste.

ERLEWINE: We are certainly not using it [now] and it hasn't been used in recent years for burying any waste. We ship waste, as you know to . . . Idaho. The nature of these wastes, I think, from the information I now have is that it is a matter of contamination of oils or materials and not a lot of high-level materials. It has some contamination but we need to investigate more.

HOLIFIELD: If there is a situation that is bad out there and the local man out there knows about it but hasn't conveyed it to the commission, he hasn't done right.

KELLY: Mr. Holifield, I can't speak for him but I hardly believe the present area manager knew about it.

HOLIFIELD: What is your understanding—and I am asking for information now—about the location of the material you think is buried out there? Is it inside the fence?

KELLY: Some inside and some just outside. . . .

HOLIFIELD: Then they had better build a new fence if there is some outside the fence. . . . You can fence it both from inside and outside so that nobody wanders over it. Another thing is that you should very carefully go over it with geiger counters or other measuring devices to find out if it is buried deeply enough. The next thing is to find out if there is any seepage going into the streams or anything like that. . . . How long would it take you to get the facts about walking over that with a measuring device to find out if there is any seepage from the ground into the atmosphere that would be in any way unsafe or alarming?

ERLEWINE: It probably simply requires a phone call. I am confident they have done this. I can't tell you they have done it.

HOLIFIELD: Am I going to have to get on a plane and go out there and walk over it myself with a measuring device and try to read it as a layman?

KELLY [*after further discussion*]: The company took the position as I left there last Friday that if it were not for the political situation, it would still be safe to bury there. . . .

After further discussion the transcript notes: "Remainder of meeting consisted of discussion of union support for defeat of candidates who sponsored a Martell-Metzger bill in Colorado" to set up a Colorado Atomic Energy Commission that would police the excesses of Rocky Flats and other A.E.C. enterprises. (The bill died in the Colorado legislature.)

On April 14, four days after the meeting at the J.C.A.E. headquarters, workmen at Rocky Flats began removing the 1,405 drums from the main burial site, located 150 yards northwest, at Gate Nine. The work was completed May 28, and a June 2 Dow report written by R. M. Vogel of the Health Physics section states: "Ten percent of the drums had holes . . . apparently caused by rust and corrosion. . . . Many of the liquid drums developed leaks during handling or after exposure to air and sun." Vogel added that "no detectable alpha contamination was found in the soil" around the burial site.

On June 28, Local 15440 struck Dow, seeking a substantial wage increase and union participation on a company safety committee. Union leaders, including President Kelly, subsequently visited with Colorado Lieutenant Governor Mark Hogan, a Democrat who unsuccessfully challenged incumbent Republican John Love in the fall 1970 gubernatorial race. The union officials complained of unsafe practices at the plant, and Hogan wired Congressman Holifield on July 18 that the J.C.A.E. should hold a congressional investigation of safety at Rocky Flats. Hogan said that, although 1,405 barrels had been removed, more nuclear garbage remained. He charged that "Dow records are inadequate and do not reflect the precise burial pits where the nuclear material rests."

Hogan also charged that Dow had paved over soil contaminated with plutonium from leaky storage barrels. He suggested that this may be the plutonium responsible for increased contamination in Old Woman's Creek, a source of water for suburban Westminster and part of Arvada.

Holifield promptly dispatched A.E.C. inspectors for a look and on July 23 he sent an optimistic letter to the lieutenant governor. Apparently all the fears Holifield expressed during the April 10 J.C.A.E. meeting in Washington had been dispelled: "With regard to your concerns about the 'burial' sites . . . there seem to be no immediate problems or the chance of leakage of radioactivity to Old Woman's Creek from the newly paved area. . . . Since none of the evidence suggests the existence of risk to the people of the environment or the State of Colorado I see no reasons for holding hearings of operations of the Rocky Flats Plant."

Later in the summer the strike ended and Dow promised the Colorado State Department of Health that it would dig up the contaminated earth that had been paved over. Plans called for shipping the radioactive waste to an authorized A.E.C. burial ground. Dow said the job would be taken care of just as soon as a task force figured out a way to scrape up the contaminated earth without inadvertently blowing some plutonium into the Denver area.

Dr. Martell, who was still dissatisfied with the A.E.C.'s policing of the situation, continued his own soil testing into 1971. He was very worried about the ongoing plant expansion, which would create an even greater hazard to the Denver public. A further problem was new experimental data that suggested that permissible occupational exposure limits to plutonium should be slashed ten to 100 times. That, of course, would make the plant inoperable: "The only way to meet those standards would be to automate it," said Dr. Martell. He believes the only way to protect the Denver populace from the plutonium is to remove highly contaminated earth as far as six miles out from the plant. He wants radioactive hot spots scooped up and buried to prevent the radiation from being redistributed by the wind.

Dr. Martell also thinks the whole Rocky Flats operations should be moved to a remote area, because "in the not too unlikely event of a major plutonium release, the resulting plutonium contamination [of Denver] could require large-scale evacuation of the affected area, the leveling of buildings and homes, the deep plowing and removal of topsoil and an unpredictable number of radiation casualities among people exposed to the initial cloud in the more seriously contaminated areas. The human casualties and economic losses from such an eventuality would greatly overweigh the costs of relocating the plant before such an accident occurs."

Very few people are listening to Dr. Martell, not because his data are wrong, but because Rocky Flats is there, it employs a lot of people and is basic to the nuclear-weapons program. Once in a while Denverites will spot a bumper sticker on a car that reads "Colorado—Playground of the A.E.C." or hear about some University of Colorado students picketing the plant. But on Dr. Martell's advice the pickets confine themselves to the west gate. That is because the east gate is downwind from the plant stacks. It seems that Denver needs an atmospheric-test-ban treaty of its own with Rocky Flats.

CHAPTER FOUR

TESTING

> The 512 announced U.S. nuclear tests include . . . 399 . . .
> at the Nevada Test Site, 98 in the 'Pacific, 3 in the South At-
> lantic, 2 in Japan, 2 at Hattiesburg, Mississippi, 2 at Amchitka
> Island, Alaska, and one each at Alamogordo, New Mexico,
> Carlsbad, New Mexico, Farmington, New Mexico, Fallon, Ne-
> vada, Hot Creek Valley, Nevada, and Grand Valley, Colorado.
>
> —U.S. ATOMIC ENERGY COMMISSION
> NEVADA OPERATIONS OFFICE

Just before the first nuclear test at Alamogordo, Enrico Fermi
bounced about offering to bet his colleagues on the prospects of
atmospheric ignition. For, despite all the careful computations,
there was still a slight chance that man's first atomic weapon
would be his last; it might ignite the atmosphere. Fermi even of-
fered to narrow the issue with a side bet on whether the bomb
would merely incinerate New Mexico or the entire world. To
everyone's relief the Trinity shot (as the first atomic test explosion
was called) did not produce atmospheric ignition, just some fallout
that turned a few head of cattle blue with beta burns (skin turns
blue).

So it was that the atomic bomb was adjudged safe for use in
the Japanese tests. Lieutenant General Leslie Groves, chief of the
Manhattan Project, tried to persuade the Truman administration
to pick Kyoto as a target, because "it was large enough to ensure
that the damage from the bomb would run out within the city,
which would give us a firm understanding of its destructive powers. [Thus we could] gain complete knowledge of the effects of an

atomic bomb. Hiroshima was not nearly so satisfactory in this respect." But Secretary of State Henry Stimson had once visited the ancient Japanese capital of Kyoto and understood its great religious significance to the people. He removed Kyoto from the target list and the military eventually had to settle for Hiroshima and Nagasaki.

While neither of these targets was ideal, both did meet the military's prime criteria. Both towns had not been scratched by previous bombing raids, which made it possible to "assess accurately the effects [and] . . . the power of the bomb." Both drops were fully monitored and yielded vast data. After the war the A.E.C. even shared this information with Japanese experts who wanted to calculate radiation exposures among survivors of the two holocausts. American and Japanese scientists also set up an Atomic Bomb Casualty Commission (A.B.C.C.), on a hill overlooking Hiroshima, where victims could be examined. Elaborate follow-up studies were conducted by specialists from both nations, but not everyone in Hiroshima was pleased with the A.B.C.C., for the scientists were studying the effects of nuclear weapons, not treating survivors. Understandably this caused some ill will among Japanese victims of the bomb who came expecting treatment and left feeling like guinea pigs.

Numerous other victims of A.E.C. tests have shared this feeling. In 1946 a miscalculated nuclear detonation forced evacuation of Bikini atoll for 20 years. Natives dependent on fishing for their survival were told to stop fishing within 100 miles of their homes while American scientists studied the radioactive marine life. In 1954 another accident contaminated several hundred Marshall Island natives, 23 Japanese fishermen and 28 American servicemen. The natives became subjects of a classic medical investigation of radiation. Each year A.E.C. scientists returned to the islands and examined the victims. Eighteen natives eventually won free round trips to American hospitals for removal of their poisoned thyroids. As for the wounded Japanese fishermen, they would stick with their own doctors, refusing inspection by eager American physicians they believed were "interested only in research."

Surprisingly though, the scientists seemed more interested in

foreign guinea pigs than in American. While snatching every op-
portunity to observe contaminated Japanese and Marshallese, the
scientists ignored subjects closer to their hospitals and laboratories. For example, the case of those 28 servicemen contaminated
in the 1954 accident in the Marshalls has not been followed up. At
least, no one in Washington seems to have records on the men's
fate or location. The A.E.C. and the Veterans Administration
plead ignorance. Similarly, the Pentagon has no records on the
thousands of American servicemen exposed to nuclear blasts during troop maneuvers at the Nevada test site. They can't find records on some Air Force pilots who flew through mushroom
clouds on monitoring missions. They have no records on the 22
men working at a Nevada asphalt batch plant who were contaminated by a plutonium cloud accidentally blown their way from a
1963 A.E.C. "safety test." Most important, the government has
yet to make a comprehensive study of the cancer rate in Nevada
and Utah towns downwind from the Nevada test site.

No one, of course, can argue that the damage nuclear tests
have wrought on America and its territorial possessions equals the
devastation of Hiroshima and Nagasaki. But without reliable monitoring and evaluation by their own government, Americans remain defenseless against insidious radiation spewed out by these
tests. In the grand tradition of American technology these men
have spent billions to develop new models of the same old product. But they have spent peanuts to modify Electrolux vacuum
cleaners to sample air for fallout that endangers the public.

The gravity of a nuclear accident depends on where it happens. When three of our nuclear bombs fell near Palomares,
Spain, a crew of 1,000 men in white suits and blue masks spent
about two months cleaning up plutonium debris spilled by the
weapons (a fourth weapon fell into the ocean). Dirt from 265 contaminated acres was dumped into 5,000 55-gallon barrels and
shipped to South Carolina for burial at an A.E.C. dump.

But when a series of 21 "safety tests" dumps a far greater
quantity of this dangerous plutonium across 160,000 contaminated
acres in Nevada, the A.E.C. feels a cleanup is unnecessary. True,
weathering of the plutonium may push the dangerous element into

urban areas, but who is going to find this dangerous substance if the A.E.C. and its sycophants simply refuse to conduct a comprehensive soil-testing program? Will the plutonium increase the cancer rate? Perhaps, but who is ever going to spend the millions on the necessary cancer studies if the A.E.C. isn't willing to finance them? When one Utah scientist proposed to give Nevada a checkup on his own, the A.E.C.–financed Public Health Service (now the Environmental Protection Agency) made it clear he was not welcome in their domain.

This hot plutonium has a radioactive half-life of 24,400 years and is scattered over 49 separate areas on or near the 1,-350-square-mile reservation. Unlike the smog in urban air or the oil in the Santa Barbara channel, this eco-catastrophe is essentially permanent and irreversible. "Radiation safety supervision of activities in this area will be required perhaps permanently."

Surprisingly most of the hot plutonium 239 contaminating the Nevada test site comes from nonnuclear explosions. All nuclear weapons include a high-explosive component which serves as a trigger to detonate the atomic device. For safety's sake the atomic device remains unarmed until ready to be fired. But there is a remote possibility that detonation of the high explosive in a plane crash or similar mishap could accidently trigger the nuclear component.

So before a new atomic-weapon design is put into production, it is run through a "safety experiment" at the Nevada test site. Scientists deliberately stage an accident that detonates the high-explosive component of the bomb. But usually the unarmed atomic device does not fire. It simply cracks apart in a nonnuclear explosion and scatters atomic-warhead debris—including toxic plutonium 239.

Ironically the plutonium particles released in these nonnuclear "safety experiments" are as much as 1,000 times hotter than they would be after a real atomic blast. In a nuclear explosion the plutonium fallout particles are coated with dust and other blast debris which reduces their radiation intensity a thousandfold. But in a nonnuclear explosion the plutonium escapes in a relatively pure and far more potent form. The A.E.C. isn't certain how much plutonium 239 is out there on the test site and says it would not tell if it knew. But it is a safe bet that the number of particles is somewhere in the trillions. The A.E.C. believes its stabilization activities keep most of the plutonium where it is and the small amount that does waft off is harmless.

But some of the agency's biomedical experts such as Arthur Tamplin and Donald Geesaman at the Livermore Laboratory are not so sure. Their concern parallels the fears voiced about the Rocky Flats plutonium. Inhalation of just 300 of these hot plutonium particles can double the risk of lung cancer. And their studies suggest that the plutonium exposure standards being used by the A.E.C. should be cut ten to 100 times to ensure public safety.

The spread of this plutonium contamination is most dangerous to the little towns near the Nevada proving grounds such as Beatty, Alamo and Tonopah. Migration of plutonium particles could eventually lead to trouble in Las Vegas, some 65 miles away. Population in the gambling spa has zoomed from 24,000 in 1950 to 153,000 today. Talk of diverting water from Lake Mead means the desert community can grow closer and closer to the contaminated test site. And lest we forget, Nevada is the nation's fastest-growing state. Population has jumped 68.9 percent in the past ten years.

Dr. Tamplin thinks that the "uncertainties posed by the plutonium contamination suggest nothing should be developed within 50 milés of the place until a comprehensive epidemiological, soil-sampling, and ecological survey is conducted." There is also the long-range problem of plutonium particles migrating 300 miles west, over the next 100 years, to the Los Angeles area. This persuades Dr. Edward Martell, who discovered the Rocky Flats contamination, to suggest that "the best approach is to locate the hot spots, scrape up all the seriously contaminated soil and bury it." Martell feels that the situation is roughly analogous to that of Palomares: "We have to clean up now; otherwise this plutonium could pose a threat for thousands of years."

The military began attacking America and its possessions after it ran out of foreign targets. Following the Japanese surrender in 1945, Army officials hoped to use an atomic bomb to destroy the Japanese fleet. But American naval officers were quite anxious to see exactly what the new weapon would do to their own ships. So a Pentagon committee headed by Major General Curtis E. LeMay organized shots Able and Baker on a flotilla of American and captured Japanese ships anchored in the Marshall Islands. About 42,000 military men, reporters, congressmen and foreign observers were brought in on 250 ships and 150 planes to watch the first shot, on June 30, 1946. Thousands of scientists came, too, because the tests provided "a reason and a theater for studies that would have been impossible at any earlier time."

The shots proved conclusively that nuclear weapons can sink ships. Veterinarians found most of the 200 white rats and 20 pigs confined in sick bays of the ill-fated ships were killed by radiation. Experts who predicted radiation from the shots would vaporize in a mushroom cloud were surprised to find the Bikini lagoon badly contaminated. Resurvey turned up a half million tons of radioactive mud in the lagoon. The American scientists recommended no fish, mollusk or other marine animal within 100 miles of Bikini lagoon be used as food, because of contamination. The biggest tragedy of these initial postwar tests was the evacuation of Bikini for over two decades. Reoccupation could not begin until 1968, when contamination finally decreased to a level acceptable for human habitation. But even with three million dollars in American aid, it would take the Bikini natives six years to make their island habitable again.

Detonation of experimental thermonuclear devices in the Marshall Islands during 1952 and 1954 made further contributions to science. On October 31, 1952, the 10.4-megaton Mike test at Elugelab on Eniwetok atoll sent up a 130,000-foot nuclear cloud. When the radioactive smoke cleared, a helicopter reconnaissance team flew over the blast site and radioed back: "Elugelab is completely gone; nothing there but water and what appears to be a deep crater." The entire island had sunk. The blast crater was a mile in diameter, which the A.E.C. boasted was big enough to "comfortably accommodate 14 Pentagon buildings." Fallout from the Mike test was heavy, but went largely unmonitored because the winds blew it into an unpopulated expanse of the Pacific where there was no detection equipment.

This monitoring failure in 1952 led to a disaster on February 28, 1954, following detonation of shot Bravo at Bikini atoll. The device yielded 15 megatons, 1,000 times the power of the small atom bombs used at Hiroshima. The fallout might have gone unmonitored again if the predicted north winds had materialized. But, instead, high winds blew the 100,000-foot cloud eastward toward the inhabited atolls of Rongelap, Ailinginae and Rongerik, and a small Japanese fishing vessel called the *Fukuryu Maru,* or *Lucky Dragon,* that was traveling nearby. The fallout was so intense that evacuation was necessary, which prompted the A.E.C. in Washington to issue a totally false press statement on March 11: "During the course of a routine atomic test in the Marshall Islands 28 United States personnel and 236 residents were transported from neighboring atolls to Kwajalein island according to plan as a precautionary measure. These individuals were unexpectedly exposed to some radioactivity. There were no burns. All were reported well. After the completion of the atomic tests, the natives will be returned to their homes."

The statement was a lie on three counts. First, says Dr. Edward Martell, "the evacuations were according to 'plan' but the plan was not devised until after the accident occurred." Second, the victims sustained beta burns, spotty epilations of the head, skin lesions, pigment changes and scarring. And many of the natives did not feel well at all. They suffered from anorexia (appetite depression), nausea, vomiting and transient depression of the formed elements in their blood. Over the next 16 years 21 of the natives on Rongelap island would develop thyroid abnormalities and thyroidectomies would be conducted on 18 of them. All but two of the 19 children who were less than ten years old when the accident happened developed thyroid abnormalities: And two of them were dwarfed for life. The Rongelap natives were allowed to return to their island in 1957 along with 100 relatives who had been absent at the time of the accident. These unexposed natives would serve as an "excellent comparison population" for scientists from the A.E.C.'s Brookhaven (New York) laboratory who annually visit the tiny island to investigate aftereffects of the disaster. The Rongelap accident would become a classic study in the field of radiobiology.

About a month after the test the Japanese fishing boat *Lucky Dragon* returned to the small port of Yaizu. A few days later medical examination showed that the 23 crewmen had been seriously contaminated by the H-bomb detonation. Although the trawler had been 100 miles from the Bravo detonation, and outside the restricted area established for the test, the crew became quite ill. All 23 men were eventually hospitalized, first in Yaizu and then in a Tokyo hospital, where doctors found them suffering from anemia, hepatitis, extreme fatigue, appetite depression and skin ailments.

The Japanese were also worried that tuna caught by other ships in the vicinity of the test could be contaminated. A.E.C. experts said this was no problem because "any radioactivity collected in [the] test area would become harmless within a few miles and completely undetectable within 500 miles or less." Japanese inspectors condemned 457 tons of tuna gathered from 683 different tuna boats. Tuna prices dropped sharply. The fishing industry was thrown into a sharp depression and many Japanese stopped eating fish as a staple. Some markets tried to draw back customers with such signs as "EAT MISAKI TUNA" and "KEEP AWAY FROM RADIATION DANGER," but customers stayed away.

Incredibly, even as the tragedy was making the Japanese headlines, the test organization (now living on ships since the Bravo shot had contaminated and smashed their temporary housing on the islands) conducted another Bikini test on March 26. Again they gave no advance warning. Luckily no boats were in the fallout pattern this time.

To offset unfavorable publicity in Japan over the *Lucky Dragon* incident, the leaders of the American establishment mounted their characteristic counterattack. Representative W. Sterling Cole, chairman of the Joint Committee on Atomic Energy, hinted that the Japanese fishing boat had been spying on the

Bravo shot. (Cole later became the first head of the International Atomic Energy Agency.) Meanwhile, a gaggle of top U. S. officials flew to the Orient and staged a sideshow. Dr. John Morton, director of the Atomic Bomb Casualty Commission, visited the ill men in the hospital and proclaimed them in "better shape than I had expected." He predicted recovery "in two or three weeks at most." Senator John Pastore of the J.C.A.E. also predicted early recovery and complained about exaggerated press accounts of the tragedy. Merrill Eisenbud, head of the A.E.C.'s Health and Safety Laboratory, astonished Japanese experts by personally measuring contamination on the *Lucky Dragon* without even wearing protective clothing. He sucked up samples of radioactive dust off the ship with a vacuum cleaner.

One of the hospitalized crewmen died of radiation injury. On May 10, 1955, more than a year after the tragedy, the rest of the crew left the Tokyo hospital for home. Noted atomic-energy expert Ralph Lapp visited Japan to write a fine book about the tragedy and predicted that the "Yaizu fishermen have a life expectancy of about five years less than their fellow non-irradiated fishermen."

Although tests would continue in the Pacific until 1962, the A.E.C. and the Pentagon gradually began to favor use of a more convenient continental test site that had been opened at Mercury, Nevada, in 1951. The Nevada test site, "America's Outdoor Nuclear Explosives Laboratory," specializes in four sorts of tests. There are proof tests of new designs, reliability tests of stockpile weapons, effects tests to determine what nuclear blasts do to structures and animals, and safety tests to make sure weapons can't detonate through accidents.

Originally the experts figured on testing smaller devices in Nevada and bigger ones in the Pacific. But accessibility and the 1963 atmospheric test ban have combined to make Nevada the focal point of nuclear-test activity. Some critics have argued that continued testing in Nevada is stirring up that dangerous plutonium left by the "safety tests." But an agency spokesman who chauffeurs visitors to the site insists the plutonium is "nothing to worry about. That's what the test site is there for; it's not the kind of place you'd go for a picnic."

On the cutoff into the test site he points at a few rusty quonset huts baking in the desert sun. They are all that remain of Camp Desert Rock, a base for troops that maneuvered beneath mushroom clouds in the 1950s. It seems that most of the original quonsets have been dismantled and shipped to Vietnam for active duty. The test site begins in Mercury, an A.E.C. company town where all the streets are named for nuclear tests, such as Trinity, Teapot, Buster and Ranger. Most Nevada test-site employees commute from Las Vegas, but some prefer to live in Mercury trailers and cabins for a nominal sum. The only catch is that men can't have women in their rooms. Even wives must stay in women's quarters. The spokesman explains: "With all the horny men around here it is safer this way."

The one compensation in this regard is that Nye County countenances prostitution. Mercury's nearest neighbor, Lathrop Wells, boasts a bordello called the Shamrock. Owner Bill Martin considers the test site a vital market: "At shot time the work force in Mercury booms and our business skyrockets." Do the nuclear shots frighten the girls? "Not at all. They don't even think about it. In fact, there's a good chance many of the girls don't even know where they are." For personnel willing to drive a little further, Vickie's, in the town of Beatty, advertises "We proudly give S & H green stamps." And over in Ash Meadows visitors can relax because a restaurant adjacent to the bordello has a U.S. Public Health Service air sampler that will detect any dangerous radiation blowing from the site. At one point an entrepreneur tried to cash in on the Mercury work force by setting up a bordello on federal land just outside town. But the Bureau of Land Management said this did not fall within their definition of multiple use.

Just beyond Mercury is a checkpoint that controls access to the "forward area" where the testing is done. The highway dips down into Frenchman Flat, site of Nevada's first atmospheric tests. As in the Pacific, radiological safety concepts were never adequate—the difference being that Nevada accidents exposed more people. In the rush to conduct the first tests in 1951, there was not enough time to develop special equipment, so modified Electrolux vacuum cleaners served as the primary air-sampling instrument. Some of these samplers didn't work; others fouled and turned out useless data. A number of trays set out on the Nevada desert to collect fallout were blown over by the wind. Aggravating the problem were soldiers from the Army chemical corps who served as radiation monitors. After the tests, a confidential A.E.C. report complained that "none of these soldiers had ever received any previous training in any of the procedures associated with a fallout study. This problem would have not been so serious were it not for the fact that [only] four [Army personnel] were permanently assigned to the program. Each test brought a new group of operators inexperienced in proper techniques. . . . Personnel were not assigned to the [radiological safety] program until a few hours before it was necessary to dispatch them to their respective stations to perform duties in which they had been only briefly indoctrinated."

The first Americans to notice the fallout from these 1951 tests were quality-control officials of the Eastman Kodak Corporation in Rochester, New York. Some of the radioactive test debris fell onto Midwestern fields and found its way into straw used to make Kodak packaging. The radiation ruined a good deal of film and Kodak screamed. The A.E.C. subsequently promised to notify Kodak of all fallout patterns that could affect film-packaging material.

Initial Nevada tests were conducted in Frenchman Flat, but in 1953 the focus shifted to Yucca Flat. This basin, which remains a center of underground testing today, has probably been ravaged by more nuclear ordnance than any other point in the world. In careless hands the bombs dropped on Yucca could have easily defused the population bomb.

Yucca initially made the limelight March 17, 1953, when shot Annie, the first of 12 events in the Upshot-Knothole series, was detonated. It was the first nuclear detonation ever shown live on network television. On hand for the event were 1,500 Sixth Army troops and allied observers, who dug into five-foot trenches just two miles from ground zero. Twenty newsmen, ten selected by the Department of Defense and ten chosen by lot from 200 reporters present, were permitted to sit in ringside trenches. Other correspondents were forced to watch from a more distant point.

Shortly before blast time an announcement crackled over the loudspeaker system: "Good morning, gentlemen. Welcome to Yucca Flat, the valley where the tall mushrooms grow . . . you will see exactly what the survivors of Hiroshima saw in 1945. . . . You will be closer to an atomic burst than any American troops have ever been in history. You may be hurt if you do not obey orders. Face left, kneel down, look down, and stay down."

When the 16-kiloton shot detonated, the trenches shook and swayed, but *The New York Times* reported: "The blast damage and heat effects proved disappointing to many of those in the trenches who had been keyed to expect more dramatic phenomena." Navy physician Frank B. Voris "found no harmful effects from the experience. I found the men physically capable of carrying out orders after the blast. They were still alert."

After the shot, officials conducted a press tour near the blast area. But the show was abruptly cut off when one guide picked up a dangerous reading on his radiation monitor. Radiological safety teams from Fort McLellan, Alabama, also had problems. Their six-volt mobile radios failed to work because their new vehicles ran on a 24-volt ignition system. And 28,000 of their 35,000 film badges (worn by personnel to detect dangerous contamination) were defective.

Fortunately these problems were solved, because on April 25, 1953, shot Simon dumped fallout on a 4,000-square-mile area in Nevada and Utah. Mobile radiation-monitoring units were employed to spot hot vehicles the same way a policeman traps speeders with radar. Roadblocks in Las Vegas and Alamo, Nevada, and Saint George, Utah, stopped 102 hot cars and sent them to local gas stations and car washes for decontamination. In Las Vegas, for example, cars were decontaminated at the Washmobile while trucks were cleaned at Mac and Bill's service stations.

Several factors complicated the job. Many of the vehicles

were so hot that they threw monitoring equipment off scale. And in Santa Clara, Utah, a radioactive truck-weighing scale contaminated a number of vehicles. Excerpts from a log kept by radiological-safety personnel show that the cleanup after shot Simon wasn't easy:

TIME: EVENT:

11:45   Report received from mobile monitoring team no. 1 at Glendale Junction advising passage of a contaminated truck through the Glendale Service Station. Maximum reading 500 millirems per hour. [Today federal standards stipulate maximum annual radiation exposure for the general populace should not exceed 170 millirems per year. And some A.E.C. experts say that limit should be slashed tenfold.]

11:58   Test director advised that attempt be made to locate and decontaminate the truck before it reached Las Vegas.

12:20   A second truck (similar to the first one) did not stop at Glendale, but its passage was noted on the survey instrument. A third truck at Glendale reading a maximum of 400 mr/hour. First 2 trucks described as flatbed PIE [vehicles].

12:30   Message to monitor in Las Vegas instructing him to attempt to flag down two PIE flat-bed trucks enroute to Las Vegas. They are in need of washing. . . . Escort them to a truck washing station on the edge of N. Las Vegas and have them washed. Use credit card for payment.

12:40   Nevada State Highway Patrol was contacted in Las Vegas and requested to locate and hold the three trucks. . . .

13:12   . . . Westbound Greyhound bus stopped at Glendale Jct. reads 250 mr/hr outside, 100 mr/hr inside.

13:32   Mobile team 1 instructed to proceed to Las Vegas station . . . and supervise . . . decontamination [on arrival at the terminal].

13:41   Las Vegas monitor radioed . . . he had stopped the three original trucks. . . .

15:15   Report received from Las Vegas on bus. . . . Maximum reading inside . . . 160 mr/hr near the back seat.

After the contamination was reduced, the vehicles were released. When the operation was mopped up one radiation monitor recommended that, "prior to any test it should be ascertained where fallout will probably occur."

The Simon mishap did not discourage 23 congressional observers from visiting the Nevada test site the following month to view shot Harry. After the 32-kiloton blast detonated the morning of May 19, 1953, an awed Representative Victor Wickersham of Oklahoma told reporters: "We were . . . not prepared for what seemed to us an eighth wonder of the world."

The 5,000 residents of Saint George, Utah, were not prepared, either, when fallout from the shot suddenly forced them to take cover for three hours. In all, the shot dumped radioactive debris on a 12,500-square-mile area in Nevada, Utah and Arizona.

Government officials did their best to calm the public. For example, in Saint George safety monitor Frank Butrico checked out all rumors of radiation damage. People who complained of radiation sickness were told they had indigestion. When one woman cried radiation had made her goats turn blue, Butrico countered that they had picked up the strange color by rubbing up against a zinc-coated fence. But the woman insisted the blue color had appeared on the goats after a test the previous year when there was no zinc fence.

The vital part of the government's public-health survey was skipped to avoid alarming the public. Because local cows were grazing on land contaminated by fallout, there was a good chance of milk supplies becoming dangerously radioactive. But Butrico said he "was afraid it might create a disturbance should it become generally known we were collecting milk samples" from dairies for radiation analysis. So he "purchased a quart of milk from a store in town. I located the producer and in discussing his milk supply in a general way, I was able to learn that the milk I had purchased that evening was obtained from the Saint George herd" after the fallout had come down. Enroute back (to the office) stops were made in Mesquite, Bunkerville and Las Vegas to obtain more milk samples.

Without necessary data on "time of milking, milking techniques, individual producers, etc.," A.E.C. radiation safety teams from Los Alamos had a hard time evaluating the samples and deciding whether milk should be withdrawn from the market in the fallout area. The Los Alamos team reported their job was made even tougher because "no standard procedure existed for preparing milk samples and counting and . . . there were no tolerance levels for fission-product contamination of milk. In the absence of a specific tolerance level for milk contaminated with fission products, the proposed emergency value for water [was] used for comparison. On this basis it is apparent that, although significant quantities of activity were found in the milk samples collected, they did not represent a source in themselves of an internal hazard." Thus, on the basis of inadequate samples and milking data, and no procedures or standards for radiation measurements, did the A.E.C. decide that the contaminated milk was safe for human consumption.

By the time fallout from shot Climax, the final event in the Upshot-Knothole series, had cleared, it was obvious the Nevada test site was not so remote as planners had hoped. The cumulative fallout record for the series showed bad news. For example, the 14 residents of the Riverside Cabins received a lifetime radiation dose of 12,000 to 15,000 millirems in less than three months (today the maximum exposure level for the nation is 170 millirems per year. The 1,500 residents of Hurricane, Utah, picked up 7,700 millirems, and 300 citizens of Rockville, Utah, received 6,000 millirems. Not far behind were the 5,000 people in Saint George, Utah, who took in 4,750 millirems.

By early 1955 the public had pretty well forgotten the Upshot-Knothole miscalculations. The Teapot series began at the Nevada test site and a horde of civil-defense and military officials began preparing for the 29-kiloton Apple-2 shot. With the help of 150 trade associations, Survival City rose out of Yucca Flat. Houses, apartment buildings, power systems, phone links, refrigerators, frozen food—everything found in Anytown, U.S.A., was installed a few miles from ground zero. Civil-defense officials supervised the work via Thunderbirds donated by Ford. After preparations were completed, they parked the cars on Doomsday Drive and headed for cover.

When Apple-2 detonated on May 5, 1955, it vaporized nearly all of its 500-foot support tower. Armored task force Razor, which had marched in 170 miles over the California desert, immediately began shelling near ground zero with tanks and .50-caliber machine guns.

As the troops secured the target, civil-defense officials found three of the ten Survival City homes ruined by the blast. Some of the power poles snapped, cars were wrecked, but the dial phone system held up. The next day 500 newsmen and other observers were given a tour of the remains of Survival City. The civil-defense mass-feeding team cooked and served beef stew and roast beef sandwiches for lunch alfresco.

Up to 1955, the Nevada test site focused on tests that would measure weapons effect, check out a new design or confirm the reliability of a stockpile bomb. Then on November 1, 1955, the A.E.C. began the "safety experiments" that led to contamination of 250 square miles of the site. At first the tests were aimed at making certain fires or shipping accidents would not detonate the nuclear component.

In 1957 this investigation was taken a step further. What would be the consequences of a nonnuclear accident? If a nuclear bomber crashed in Spain, how far would the plutonium scatter? So on April 24, 1957, a nonnuclear explosion was staged as part of Operation Plumbbob. Scientists then went into ground zero area to (1) measure the amount of plutonium dispersed and (2) practice decontamination.

Subsequent studies proved that winds could pick up plutonium particles and spread contamination. So in 1963 "Project Rollercoaster" was organized on the Tonopah Test Range and the Nellis Bombing and Gunnery Range of the Nevada test site. American and British experts set up an elaborate monitoring network to measure plutonium dispersal from four nonnuclear events. Plans also called for exposing 300 dogs, sheep and burros to a plutonium cloud. Subsequent sacrifice would pinpoint the animals' radiation exposure.

Unfortunately accidents can happen, even during "safety experiments." Following detonation of the first Rollercoaster shot, on May 15, 1963, a wind shift swept the dangerous plutonium cloud over Scotty's Junction, Lathrop Wells, Lida Junction and Beatty, Nevada, as well as Death Valley Junction, California. Hardest hit were 22 men working at an asphalt batch plant 32 miles northwest of Beatty.

The U. S. Public Health Service, while pointing out that the exposure did not exceed federal limits (limits that are now being restudied by the Environmental Protection Agency) was seriously concerned. It recommended that, after future "safety experiment" accidents, "thought should be given to people farther downwind; they might be moved before maximum [plutonium] cloud levels arrive."

Since the limited test-ban treaty was signed on August 5, 1963, all safety experiments and nuclear-weapons tests have been conducted underground. In retrospect, scientists such as the A.E.C.'s Dr. Arthur Tamplin think "the tests should have been conducted underground to start with. The safety experiments could have also gone underground or been simulated in a laboratory."

But even the underground shots create hazards, by venting radiation through fissures and causing small earthquakes.

Sixteen of the 200 announced underground shots since the test ban have vented radiation which has blown off the test site. Twelve other tests have vented radiation detectable beyond the immediate vicinity of the firing point, but not off the test site. In addition forty other underground tests have vented some radioactivity in the immediate vicinity of the firing point. This means that sixty-eight of the 200 announced underground tests have vented. About 100,000 dollars worth of seismic damage claims have been paid for broken windows and cracked plaster to victims such as Caesar's Palace in Las Vegas. About the only person in Nevada to make a significant stand against the test site was Howard Hughes, who tried to prevent a big underground shot in the spring of 1968.

Hughes appealed directly to Vice-President Humphrey for cancellation, but the shot went off as planned. It is hard to argue with Nevada's largest single employer, which provides jobs for 7,300 and a payroll over 100 million dollars. When Hughes finally left Nevada, in December of 1970, rumor had it that one of his reasons was fear of further A.E.C. tests.

Whether or not this is true, his timing was certainly good. On December 18, 1970, 20-kiloton shot Baneberry vented in one of the worst underground-test mishaps in A.E.C. history. The accident forced evacuation of 600 workers, 300 of whom were contaminated. Eighty cars were also held for decontamination and the owners were rented vehicles in the interim. A work camp in the forward area of the test site was badly contaminated. It was two months before it was safe for reoccupation and five months before the agency approved resumption of new underground tests under supposedly tighter safety standards. Radiation from the December 16 venting was detected in 12 Western states. The A.E.C. assured the public that all the contamination was well within established limits and said that milk samples were collected "not because there was a health hazard, but for purposes of documentation." Howard Hughes probably chuckled when he heard that one.

CHAPTER FIVE

DEFENSE

When the new nuclear-weapons series have passed their tests in Nevada, production models are deployed to hundreds of sites at home and abroad. Virtually every major city in the United States has some nuclear weapons nearby. They can be found at Strategic Air Command bases, Air Defense Command bases, Army Strike Command bases, Polaris missile-assembly facilities, naval ammunition depots, naval weapons stations, and antiaircraft missile sites.

Deploying so many bombs over such a widespread area poses many hazards. The possibility of sabotage increases, more people are forced to live with bombs in the neighborhood and potential enemies have a broader range of nuclear stockpile targets. The Pentagon relies on two principal systems to defend our weapons. The first is garrison-style security around the stockpile sites that wards off ground invasion. The second is a mammoth international defense system called North American Aerospace Defense Command, which protects against air attack.

Publicly the leaders of the weapons program express complete confidence in stockpile security. The Air Force's Manzano base, outside Albuquerque, is touted as the model stockpile. When critics raise fears about the safety of our nuclear weapons, the experts point to four fences, security guards and patrols that supposedly make this, the nation's largest stockpile site, impenetrable. At least, this was the story until January 25, 1971, when two young Mexicans somehow managed to crack the Manzano security system. When the Mexicans were apprehended, the military's first move was to find a Spanish translator to ask the young men how they got past the electrified fences and barbed wire. The trespassers said they had thought Manzano was a large, rich ranch where they could get food and employment. They were promptly deported, but Manzano officials refused to tell how the Mexicans broke into the nuclear garrison. It was explained that giving details of the trespass would be revealing classified security matters.

The Pentagon also insists our nuclear weapons stored in foreign sites are secure. But certain congressmen are not convinced. On May 26, 1970, Senator Stuart Symington, chairman of the Foreign Relations Subcommittee on U.S. Security Agreements and Commitments Abroad, discussed this question with General David A. Burchinal, Deputy Commander-in-Chief of U. S. Forces in Europe. Senator Symington spoke of nuclear weapons America has placed all over the world: "In my opinion, at least, in some places, we do not guard them properly; and that is based on actual experience plus letters I have received."

The Pentagon is far more concerned about enemy attack than about enemy thieves. That is why much of its defense budget is spent on NORAD, which protects the weapons and 220 million Americans and Canadians with a staff of 114,000 personnel at 300 locations. The headquarters is ENT Air Force Base in downtown Colorado Springs, Colorado. The base does not look like the heart of North American Aerospace Defense. The main five-story building is a former tuberculosis sanitarium that could be ravaged with a few Molotov cocktails. The subordinate white wooden office buildings look as if they could be leveled with a sonic boom. Luckily there are no sonic booms around ENT because it is the nation's only Air Force base without its own airport.

The prestige and power of ENT is found by taking a 13-mile

drive south of town to Cheyenne Mountain, a Rocky Mountain front-range citadel and neighbor to lofty Pikes Peak.

Cheyenne Mountain is known as the home of the Broadmoor Hotel complex, the Will Rogers Shrine and a municipal zoo and ski area. It also nestles the world's biggest fallout shelter, a 143-million-dollar subterranean complex that serves as NORAD command post. The facility rests beneath 1,500 feet of granite and is designed to give NORAD a bombproof, fast-reacting headquarters that could "button up" from the rest of the world and coordinate a nuclear war for 30 days, assuming the enemy attack is not too hard. About 750 men in 11 separate steel buildings would call the shots under the direction of the President. Information from the one-billion-dollar radar systems that feed into the mountain's 14 computers would provide the decisive information on how to run World War III.

During the summer of 1970 construction crews went to work on a 20.8-million-dollar addition. They began erecting three steel buildings in underground caverns. When the construction is done, the buildings will be furnished with computers, communication equipment, and power systems to run the new Safeguard (A.B.M.) system. Privately some military men wonder about the wisdom of running A.B.M. or any other part of the nuclear-weapons system from this cave. Generals and engineers, as well as professors and scientists, point out that Cheyenne Mountain was built in another age, that it could be out of date, that modern nuclear weaponry could even collapse the mountain and destroy the command post. In short, nuclear proliferation makes A.B.M. headquarters obsolete before it is finished.

These are sober thoughts that never occurred to ambitious American communities that bid for the NORAD control center during the mid-1950s. In those days the Army was obsessed with the notion of building "hardened" facilities, i.e., subterranean structures shielded with concrete and steel. No missile silo or fall-out shelter was worth anything to defense planners unless it was "hardened" against enemy attacks. So the Army Corps of Engineers surveyed the nation and narrowed original contenders down to three sites in the Colorado Springs area. Then, as Army Colonel H. G. Woodbury explained: "We conducted extensive drilling operations both vertical and horizontal, extending 1,200 to 2,300 feet into the mountains and valley floor to learn what materials God had used to mold this part of our world. We also made comparative cost estimates and finally picked 9,300-foot Cheyenne Mountain."

The military broke ground in 1961 and four years, 1.1 million pounds of explosives, 90,000 cubic yards of rock, 90,000 rock bolts, 42,000 cubic yards of concrete and 7,000 tons of steel later, Cheyenne Mountain was opened—or closed—depending on how you look at it.

In the pioneer days all personnel had to walk a third of a mile into the tunnel to reach their jobs. Everyone wore hard hats for protection from rocks and had to dodge puddles, carry flashlights and keep candles ready for periodic blackouts inside the office. Occasional snowstorms kept everyone in overnight. Two 25-ton steel blast doors located 50 feet apart form the crucial airlock for protection against nuclear attack. Betty M. Ireland, the first NORAD secretary to work inside the mountain, remembers: "At first the blast doors would get stuck all the time. Once we were trapped between them for half an hour and some of the men were really frightened. There was one personnel man downtown who would always call up and make sure the doors were working before coming over for a visit."

Blast-door failure has embarrassed NORAD officials. Classic stories circulate in military circles about brass visiting Cheyenne Mountain for an inspection only to find themselves locked out by malfunctioning blast doors. In the event of national emergency the blast doors would be sealed or "buttoned up" to safeguard the Combat Operations Center. But frequently the doors are unbuttoned to facilitate maintenance work. Of course, this is done only on days when no one at NORAD expects nuclear wars.

Visitors to NORAD always begin with the traditional press briefing, The NORAD Story. A handout explains that "since late 1963 the NORAD briefing team has presented The NORAD Story more than 1,200 times to live audiences," a fact confirmed by the lackluster delivery of the briefing officers. In essence, the military spokesman report that the Russians are coming at America with SLBM (Submarine-Launched Ballistic Missiles) called Sark-Serb, and Golem; aircraft called Bear, Badger, Bison and Blinder, capable of firing Kangaroo, Kipper and Kitchen missiles; and ballistic missiles called Sandal, Scamp, SS-9, SS-11 and SS-13. The Russians are also working on two war satellites called FOBS and MOBS.

Presently the United States can defend only against Soviet bombers. It has no protection against Soviet ICBMs or SLBMs. Even American Minutemen ICBMs are vulnerable. This is where the Safeguard system comes in. The ABMs Spartan and Sprint missiles will protect America's ICBMs from Russia's ICBMs. NORAD officials say that Spartan and Sprint carry nuclear warheads: "This is an important advantage, for the nuclear warhead has a wide bursting range capable of destroying a target without a direct hit."

This wide bursting range is one reason why nuclear weapons are so popular with the American military. There has been, over the years, a continual accuracy problem with new weapons systems. For example, M.I.T. engineering professor J. C. R. Licklider reviewed the first Air Force tests of the F-86, F-89 and F-94. Here is what happened the first time each aircraft fired rockets at a towed target: "The F-86 had a malfunction of the rocket launcher: no hits. The F-94 rockets disturbed the air intake of the jet engines and caused a flame-out: no hits. The F-89 fired all its 104 rockets: 103 went off at an angle of about 45 degrees from the line to the target; one rocket wobbled erratically, departed from the others, and by the sheerest of flukes scored a direct hit on target." Obviously, though, this terrible sort of inaccuracy is irrelevant if the warhead if equipped with a nuclear weapon—even a wide miss can still knock out the enemy with far-reaching radiation.

Another rationale for Safeguard is that it will make up for computerized weapons systems that do not always work. One Budget Bureau study of 13 major Air Force/Navy aircraft and missile programs worth 40 billion dollars shows that less than 40 percent of the systems performed acceptably. Four programs worth 12 billion dollars were canceled or phased out and five other programs worth 13 billion dollars performed poorly—electronic reliability less than 75 percent of initial specifications.

This kind of difficulty plagues the men of Cheyenne Mountain. Communications are the backbone of the center; 10,000 circuits extending over 16 million circuit miles end in the mountain. One of the crucial systems that men in the Combat Operations Center rely on is the Ballistic Missile Early Warning Systems— one billion dollars' worth of long-range, ultra-high-speed radars that watch for surprise missile attacks over the top of the world. NORAD officials boast that data gleaned from space and automatically sent to the Colorado Springs headquarters in microseconds makes BMEWS the "bulwark against the intercontinental ballistic missile." Alas, accidents do happen. Early in its operational life BMEWS detected an "incoming ballistic missile" that turned out to be the moon. Luckily the error was caught in time, no counterstrike was ordered and a world war was called off.

NORAD officials have also had problems with their National Warning Center, which flashes national-emergency messages to broadcast outlets across the nation. Every Saturday the center runs a test of the alert message with a computer tape that breaks directly into the broadcast wires of the Associated Press and United Press International. On Saturday, February 20, 1971, NORAD teletype operator W. S. Eberhardt picked up the wrong tape and flashed an authenticated national-emergency message to 2,500 stations across the nation. Some went off the air, others were skeptical and did nothing. Others, such as KNBR in San Francisco, which is supposed to coordinate local broadcast activities during a national emergency, did not even see the message until over a half hour after it came on the wire. After 40 minutes and three attempts the NORAD operators finally got the proper deactivating code over the wire. The A.P. and U.P.I. subsequently decided NORAD would no longer be allowed to break into the wires on Saturday mornings. The warning center was instructed to send its messages to the wire-service headquarters in New York, where they would be screened for errors and then passed on to the stations.

Accidents like these lend credence to the cries of critics who believe that computerized defense systems will never work. One is Daniel D. McCracken, who has written ten books on computer programming. He says that computer control of the ABM could succeed only if tested "under actual operating conditions over a period of years." Short of actual nuclear-combat exercises in the atmosphere, there is no way of knowing the results of the programs that will be fed into the computers. He points out that the Army has worked on a computerized inventory system for several years and is two and a half years behind schedule: "This is about one hundredth as hard as programming the Safeguard ABM and is child's play by comparison." McCracken believes that if Russia gave the United States its Intercontinental Ballistic Missile attack plan for April 1974, "I doubt we'd have time to program ABM to stop very many of them. The enemy knows that the simplest way to make sure our ABM system would always be useless would be to keep forcing changes in our computer programs. All such things have to be anticipated in writing the computer programs. When a new offensive threat is detected [by us], writing the ABM programs to respond to it is a matter of months and years of work."

The men who run Cheyenne Mountain refuse to discuss such criticisms. They continue building the ABM center in the belief that it will keep the peace. Indeed, General Norman L. Magnuson, deputy director of the Combat Operations Center, reports that pacifism runs rampant at NORAD: "Some of the most peaceful people you can find are in uniform. Our people are doing their best to avoid war. Some of us have fought in wars and we know how terrible they can be. Of course, we're not naïve, we know that some conflict is inevitable. African tribes fight, there are Vietnams and there will probably be more Vietnams. But we believe we can deter a big war." Deterrence is the basic NORAD strategy. As NORAD policy states: "Deterrence means simply to be so strong that any would-be enemy knows an attack by him would be defeated so he stays home." Since the Combat Operations Center has never been through a real war, regular test exercises are run to keep NORAD strong. Among the code names used during the tests are Fade Out, Double Take, Round House, Cocked Pistol, Big Noise, Snow Man, Lemon Juice and Apple Jack.

No one likes being locked up in the mountain for these three- or four-day test exercises. Colonel Edward F. Fletcher says: "It's not very comfortable sleeping in bunks and being kept from the rest of the world. There really isn't anything to do but sleep, work or eat."

Eating is the major compensation for Cheyenne Mountain workers. In fact this could be the only military installation in the world where no one complains about the food. A diverse menu under the supervision of Sergeant Don D. Baker surpasses all expectations. The kitchen is provisioned to feed employees for a month-long emergency "button up." But Sergeant Baker says: "After 30 days, God help us all."

It would be inaccurate to say that soldiers view a tour of duty in Cheyenne Mountain as a dream assignment. On the other hand, few whiners work in the Combat Operations Center. The officers believe Cheyenne Mountain is a lot better than working in Thule, Greenland, or Vietnam.

Brass do their best to make soldiers feel at home inside the windowless offices. Walls are covered with traditional military posters about good grooming and security. One reads: "Keep America Beautiful. Get A Proper Haircut." Another says: "If He Doesn't Have A Need To Know, You Should Tell Him Where To Go."

A sauna bath and exercise room offer a chance for relaxation and a complete clinic offers medical and dental care. The mountain also comes equipped with its own water, heating, sewage disposal and decontamination system. There is also a base exchange, snack bar, barber shop and police department.

Secretary Betty Ireland says: "People are always asking us what our families would do if we were buttoned up inside the mountain during a wartime situation. Military people have their families trained for emergencies. After all, this is a way of life for us. My kids know what to do, the sixteen-year-old knows where the closest fallout shelter is. And I've told my children that if the end should come, their mother will have the biggest tombstone in the world, a mountain of solid granite."

Tombstone talk is not the kind of thing the men at NORAD like to get into. One sergeant says, "People think that once the bomb is dropped, it's all over. This kind of doomsday talk is silly. Even in an all-out war many parts of the U. S. would be safe."

But there is no assurance that Colorado Springs or Cheyenne Mountain would be among the survivors in nuclear war. In exchange for anonymity, one general agreed to a frank discussion of nuclear reality. He says: "When Cheyenne Mountain was excavated for the NORAD headquarters a decade ago, most military men believed a fortified underground center was the safest command post. The Combat Operations Center was built to withstand any known nuclear attack. But today the Soviets have developed massive new 20-megaton nuclear weapons called the SS-9 that could cave in the mountain."

Atomic Energy Commission studies show that a 20-megaton nuclear device can crater out an area to a depth of 1,000 feet. Thus two direct hits on the mountain would dig far beyond the 1,500-foot depth of the underground headquarters.

The general explains: "That's why some top military men now argue that you can't achieve survivability in a single fixed command post; the enemy can concentrate its fire and dig it out. It's beginning to look like true survivability can only be achieved with an airborne command post like the Strategic Air Command's 'Looking Glass.' Because it's always moving, the Looking Glass aircraft is probably safer than the mountain. Nonetheless the Colorado Springs cave remains a good second choice command post.

"Of course, with the ABM addition, Cheyenne Mountain becomes a bigger target.

"The best defense would be to dig out another, deeper installation. I think we'd be a lot safer if we dug down deeper than 1,500 feet, say maybe to 5,000 feet below the earth [surface]. But that would probably be too expensive. So I guess we're just going to have to pray that we don't have any big nuclear wars, just small ones. Of course, I'm not too worried about the men in Cheyenne Mountain. We've equipped them with bulldozers and I think they can dig themselves out."

CHAPTER SIX

OFFENSE

"Folks, this is your pilot. We'll be landing in Albuquerque in about five minutes. Those of you on the right side of the aircraft should have a good view of Manzano Mountain, America's largest nuclear-weapons storage site. On our final approach we'll be going in over Sandia Laboratory, Sandia Atomic Museum, the Pentagon's Nuclear Weapons School, and Stockpile Management Center. From there we'll head on in to the Albuquerque airport, which doubles as Kirtland Air Force Base, where a lot of nuclear weapons training and research is done. Make sure your seat belts are fastened. Please extinguish all cigarettes and there's no smoking until you are well inside the terminal building."

None of the commercial pilots who fly thousands of passengers into Albuquerque every day has ever given an announcement like this. But they could, because Albuquerque is headquarters for America's nuclear offense. Give most Americans a mushroom cloud–shaped ink blot on a Rorschach test and they'd probably associate it with disaster. But the average Albuquerque resident would probably identify it with a paycheck. For the mushroom cloud is the symbol for 15,000 people who make 180 million dollars each year in the town's biggest industry, nuclear weapons.

78

The mushroom cloud is found on shoulder patches, signs and maps alike, and points to Sandia Base, headquarters for the American nuclear business.

Here giant computers keep track of our nuclear stockpile. Technical writers turn out thick manuals on the care and feeding of nuclear weapons. Soldiers learn how to clean up after an atomic accident. Biologists and physicians figure out the safest way to fight in fallout. College professors help the Air Force design bases that can withstand nuclear attack. Even chaplains are taught how to adapt themselves to troop needs.

Running the nuclear offense is the job of all the weapons-oriented agencies around Sandia. The A.E.C.'s Albuquerque operations office oversees the production empire. The Sandia Corporation makes and tests nonnuclear components. The Air Force runs Manzano and a special (nuclear) weapons laboratory. The Defense Nuclear Agency manages the stockpile, researches nuclear-warfare problems, writes technical manuals and coordinates the needs of the Pentagon with the A.E.C. A flock of research spin-offs help study the biological effects of nuclear weapons nearby.

The prime job of all these agencies is to perpetuate the notion that nuclear warfare can be run efficiently, humanely and successfully. They say all it takes is proper research and training. Thus the nuclear soldiers are trained much like other professionals. They must come to D.N.A. school at Sandia to learn how to use bombs. They must practice assembling and disassembling nuclear weapons and learn the proper diet for nuclear war.

To get this information for the offensive team, the agency has sponsored a wide variety of nuclear research that has scorched pigs, blinded rabbits and deafened Dalmatians. They have used terminal-cancer patients to find out how much radiation a soldier can absorb before he becomes "combat ineffective." They have run troops through nuclear maneuvers and studied the psychological effects.

Training to become a nuclear soldier has traditionally begun at Sandia's Nuclear Weapons School.

Begun in 1946, Sandia has a staff of 200 which teaches 25 different courses listed in a 92-page catalog to servicemen from around the world. Instruction ranges from a two-hour orientation on nuclear weapons to a year-long course for medical officers. In these classrooms soldiers learn how to arm, disarm, package, inspect, test, maintain, clean, preserve, paint, package and mark weapons. There are even courses to train people how to handle nuclear weapons involved in aircraft crashes, vehicular accidents, storage accidents, isolated weapon impact, Nike-Hercules accidents and multicarrier collision.

Even God gets into the curriculum in the "Chaplains Nuclear Training Course." The scope of instruction includes: "General orientation in the characteristics and capabilities of nuclear weapons and their effects; authoritative presentations on the medical and psychiatric aspects of nuclear warfare; consideration of the moral and ethical principles involved in nuclear research and the employment of nuclear weapons; discussions of troop reaction and the adaptation of the chaplain's function to nuclear disaster."

Another big job at Albuquerque is preparation of technical manuals that accompany all nuclear weapons as they are deployed around the world. Naturally these manuals must be complete, accurate and easy for soldiers to understand. In Washington, D.N.A.'s director L. M. Mustin says: "When a new weapon with all its technical publications comes out, we sort of drive it through our boys at a site to see if the instructions are soldier-proof, sailor-proof, or airman-proof—to see if they can understand what they are supposed to do and do it right."

How is this done? "By handing them the weapon and handing them the instructions and saying, 'Here you are, fellows, go to it.' . . . Then [if] there's something wrong with the instructions, we go back to the drawing boards and rewrite a little bit." This sort of correction is quite common, "little improvements, clarification here, change the word there, that sort of thing."

Much of the material studied in class deals with the special medical problems of nuclear war. To help commanders use their troops most effectively, the Pentagon sponsors a wide variety of research on combat effectiveness during nuclear war. The implications of this research are published in various service manuals. These documents suggest some very special problems facing our nuclear offense. One of the biggest is figuring out what can be expected from soldiers who have been exposed to varying degrees of radiation. Chart A from the Army's *Handbook for Medical Service Personnel* shows what happens to soldiers with various degrees of radiation injury. Thus soliders who receive less than 200 rads (the basic unit of absorbed dose of ionizing radiation) are considered combat effective. Soldiers who receive 200 to 600 rads can perform routine tasks but sustained combat activities are hampered for six to 20 hours. Soldiers who receive over 1,000 rads would be largely incapacitated except for an early capability of heroic response. The region of instant death is expected to be over 50,000 rads. Recommended therapy includes sedatives, antibiotics, blood transfusions and "reassurance." Chart B indicates the probability of casualties for troops at various distances from different weapons. Thus troops wearing summer uniforms would stand a 50 percent chance of second-degree burns if they are within 580 meters of a one-kiloton airburst. The burn risk is slightly increased if they are wearing winter uniforms.

All this data is used for "command radiation guidance" to help officers predict combat effectiveness of contaminated troops. During the first one to three hours after significant exposure the troops will probably not be combat effective since they will be busy vomiting. And then what? Well, the officer should figure out whether or not a contaminated soldier is capable of doing his job. The manual suggests officers base their decision on these estimates of physical effectiveness necessary to perform typical military combat tasks: (*a*) fire a preplaced weapon, 10 percent; (*b*) operate radio communications, 20 percent; (*c*) drive a vehicle, 50 percent; (*d*) aim a weapon, 80 percent; (*e*) assault a position, 90 percent; (*f*) hand-to-hand combat, 90 percent.

Of course, the Army manual realizes that the enlightened commander treats the individual soldier as merely a part of the big picture: "Although individual effectiveness may be of concern, command elements at higher levels are more likely to be interested in effectiveness of units rather than individuals. . . . It has been estimated that ten to 30 percent ineffectiveness in a unit may render that unit incapable of accomplishing its mission. However, it

ACUTE CLINICAL EFFECTS OF SINGLE HIGH DOSE RATE

Dose (Range)		0–100 rads (subclinical range)	100–1000 rads (sublethal range)	
			100–200 rads	200–600 rads
INITIAL PHASE	Incidence of nausea and vomiting	NONE	5–50%	50–100%
	Time of onset		Approx. 3–6 hrs.	Approx. 2–4 hrs.
	Duration		Less than 24 hrs.	Less than 24 hrs.
	Combat effectiveness	100%	100%	Can perform routine tasks. Sustained combat or comparable activities hampered for 6–20 hrs.
LATENT PHASE	Duration		More than 2 weeks.	Approx. 7–15 days.
SECONDARY PHASE	Signs and symptoms	NONE	Moderate leukopenia.	Severe leukopenia; purpura, hemorrhage; infection; epilation about 300 rads.
	Time of onset post exposure.		2 weeks or more.	Several days to 2 weeks.
	Critical period post exposure.		NONE	4–6 weeks.
	Organ system responsible.	NONE		Hematopoietic tissue.
HOSPITALIZATION	Percentage	NONE	Less than 5%	90%
	Duration		45–60 days.	60–90 days.
INCIDENCE OF DEATH		NONE	NONE	0–80%
AVERAGE TIME OF DEATH				3 weeks to 2 months.
THERAPY		NONE	Reassurance, hematologic surveillance.	Blood transfusion, antibiotics.

EXPOSURES OF WHOLE-BODY IRRADIATION TO HEALTHY ADULTS

100–1000 rads (sublethal range)	Over 1,000 rads (lethal range)	
600–1,000 rads	1,000–3,000 rads	over 3,000 rads
75–100%	100%	
Approx. 1–2 hrs.	Less than 1 hr.	
Less than 48 hrs.	Less than 48 hrs.	Approx. 48 hrs.
Can perform only simple routine tasks. Significant incapacitation in upper part of range. Lasts more than 24 hrs.	Progressive incapacitation following an early capability for intermittent heroic response.	Progressive incapacitation following an early capability for intermittent heroic response.
None to approx. 7 days.	None to approx. 2 days.	NONE
Severe leukopenia; purpura, hemorrhage; infection; epilation about 300 rads.	Diarrhea; fever; disturbance of electrolyte balance	Convulsions; tremor; ataxia; lethargy
Several days to 2 weeks.	2–3 days.	
4–6 weeks.	5–14 days.	1–48 hrs.
Hematopoietic tissue.	Gastrointestinal tract.	Central nervous system.
100%	100%	100%
90–120 days.	2 weeks.	2 days.
90–100%	90–100%	
3 weeks to 2 months.	1–2 weeks.	2 days.
Blood transfusion, antibiotics.	Maintenance of electrolyte balance.	Sedatives.

Chart B

COMPARISON OF WEAPON EFFECTS (AIRBURST)

Casualty Criteria	Yield			
	1 KT	*10 KT*	*100 KT*	*1 MT*
	(Distance in meters)			
50% probability of serious wounds (glass fragments)	740	1,610	3,860	8,530
50% probability of lethality or displacement impact	450	1,130	2,900	7,080
Foxhole collapse (50% filling)	270	580	1,260	2,730
2° burns on exposed surfaces	805	2,415	6,440	17,700
2° burns—50% probability under summer uniform	580	1,480	3,700	9,330
2° burns—50% probability under winter uniform	515	1,200	3,380	8,370
650 Rads (Nausea and vomiting within 4 hours)	840	1,290	1,770	2,570
3000 Rads (Nausea and vomiting within 1 hour)	580	970	1,530	2,090

is not always a matter of how many ineffectives there are in a unit so much as who these casualties are."

Fortunately there should be plenty of time to evaluate the casualties because "the combination of variations in exposure and biological response makes sudden, simultaneous loss of all personnel in a unit unlikely. Generally, the unit commander and the surgeon should have ample time to evaluate unit effectiveness as individuals become sick." The unit surgeon is expected to offer medical and moral advice to the commander about the risk of fighting in an area contaminated by fallout: "He can emphasize that at 200 rads the commander will pay a severe casualty price for an objective; and at 800 rads a severe mortality price." For contemplated exposure a table is given to help the surgeon get a "general impression of the unit's ability to perform a particular mission," which can be supplemented with observation of the unit's "past and present performances, observing the rate of sick call and observing the type and number of symptoms."

Diet is another important concern of the medical officers. They should make sure unpackaged foods contaminated by fallout are washed and trimmed. Flour, sugar and salt should be set aside to allow natural radioactivity to decay to acceptable levels: "If food supplies are critically low, contaminated food may have to be consumed. In this event it may be advisable to dilute the contamination by mixing with uncontaminated food. This will reduce the total amount of radioactivity to a level where exposure will be minimal."

"Food animals such as cattle, hogs, goats, sheep, and poultry that have been exposed to fallout should be considered fit for consumption and slaughtered using routine procedures. Mild radiation sickness in animals does not necessarily mean that they cannot be used for food. Even if the animals have been exposed to an internal radiation hazard, they can still be used as food as long as the internal organs are discarded during butchering. Chickens that have eaten radioactive materials may lay contaminated eggs, but most of the radioactivity will be concentrated in the shells. The white and yolks will be free of significant radiation and can be eaten without harm. It is probable that chickens will not lay if the radioactive body burden is large enough that their eggs are unfit to eat."

This nuclear offense strategy is largely based on hard scientific data generated by Pentagon medical research. Much of it is generated by the Defense Nuclear Agency, which spends about 4.2 million dollars each year for studies on the biomedical, biophysical and psychological effects of radiation injury. The D.N.A.-sponsored Armed Forces Radiobiology Institute in Bethesda, Maryland, does a good deal of the work, but some of it is contracted out to experts at universities and medical research centers.

During the early 1950s troops were actually able to play nuclear war games beneath the fallout clouds in Nevada. Armored convoys, ground troops and Air Force squadrons also practiced mopping up ground-zero operations. For example, the Human Resources Research Organization found that "men who learned a substantial number of facts from the [pretest] indoctrination were more likely than other men to become self-confident and willing to volunteer for potentially hazardous duty." But while these experiments did yield some information on the psychological impact of nuclear warfare, they did not help answer the medical uncertainties.

Ideally the test organization would have liked to expose soldiers to big doses of radiation and to study the medical effects. Obviously this was morally unacceptable. Animals were used instead, but yielded little data. During the spring of 1957 D.N.A.'s predecessor, the Armed Forces Special Weapons Project asked the A.E.C. to drop a stockpile weapon of a known nuclear yield near 700 animals. The A.E.C. agreed, but A.F.S.W.P. encountered a number of problems. Finding 700 suitable animals was difficult. Dogs were immediately ruled out because of the A.S.P.C.A.. Goats were rejected because their hair would catch fire from the heat of the blast. Someone suggested shaving the goats before the test, but that idea was rejected because it seemed likely the goats would freeze while waiting for the blast. Donkeys seemed like a good choice but 700 were not available. Finally pigs were chosen on the assumption that they would react to the test much like humans. So the Pentagon bought 700 pigs and shipped them to the Nevada test site's Frenchman Flat, where they were field-tested in every conceivable way. One study involved stationing pig platoons at various distances from the contemplated ground zero to calculate lethality. Other pigs were put into foxholes and slit trenches to see if these positions would offer some protection from the bomb.

Another experiment studied the bomb's blast effects, mainly the bomb's power to break up battlefield equipment into flying metal fragments that would kill or maim soldiers. A group of pigs were penned up amidst a pile of typical battlefield litter such as canteens, ammunition, ammunition boxes, helmets, rifles, etc. Another pig group was placed in front of windowpanes so the experts could calculate damage from flying glass. Nearby control pigs were placed inside special aluminum pork barrels that would shield them from the blast (metal and glass) debris that would strike their brethren. After the tests the experts compared the shielded and unshielded pigs.

Perhaps the most carefully constructed study was the one aimed at estimating what a nuclear blast would do to human skin. The scientists figured the pigs would be perfect for this because their skin is similar to man's. But after due consideration it was concluded that naked pigs were unacceptable. They had to be clothed like humans. So special Army khaki uniforms were tailored for the pigs. Unforeseen technical delays forced a six-week delay in the shot. During the waiting period the pigs gained weight and split their seams. This forced the experts to sew a second, more ample set of clothes for the animals.

Finally on June 24, 1957, the weather was right for 37-kiloton shot Priscilla. The pigs slept as the predawn countdown began. Nearby a team of 12 Army surgeons prepared for treating casualties in a nearby specially equipped evacuation hospital. The surgeons were on hand to practice triage (medical management of mass casualties). After the blast they planned to classify pigs into treatment priorities that would benefit the largest number. The wounded would be sorted into those who could survive with immediate surgery and those who could survive with surgery that could be delayed. The fatally injured would be abandoned to leave time for operating on potential survivors.

The official number of pigs killed by 37-kiloton shot Priscilla on that June morning is a Pentagon secret. But surgeons who were there do concede that pigs either survived the blast or they didn't. Prompt medical attention seemed to make little difference. The doctors had expected to operate on some 500 pigs, but when the wounded pigs were brought in from the field via ambulance, the senior medical officer found that only seven needed surgery. The pigs turned out to be much tougher than humans. The uniformed animals used in the skin-burn experiment survived remarkably well. Unlike humans, who can die with second-degree burns over 50 percent of their bodies, the pigs were able to take 80 percent third-degree wounds and survive.

As long as the pigs' snouts and feet were not burned, they were able to walk to food and survive. The pigs also turned out to have tougher abdomens than humans. Glass and metal fragments that probably would have killed or seriously injured humans did not hurt the pigs. Broken bones were few and subsequent expectation of wound infections did not materialize. When the test was over, some of the healthy pig survivors were shipped back to Walter Reed Medical Center in Bethesda, Maryland, where their progress was followed up for several years.

Colonel Ed Huycke, who was a member of the pig surgical team in 1957 and is now chief of the D.N.A. Medical Directorate in Washington, says, "What we learned from this experiment was that field testing is not the way to go. Afterwards we decided it would be much better to start simulating these nuclear combat questions in laboratories, or to use human subjects when possible." The Priscilla pig experiment has become something of an underground classic inside the nuclear medical fraternity. The Pentagon is so ashamed that it will not even consider letting writers inspect the various reports that were written on the test. D.N.A. Director Mustin says: "These reports are not classified, or anything. I'm just not going to let them out. The entire experiment was a terrible flop and it would be too embarassing to let the details out."

Like the pig tests, some of the initial experiments aimed at calculating retinal damage from nuclear fireballs were disappointing. These tests were conducted to learn how to protect our flight crews against the flash of their own weapons being delivered in a planned attack at night. The light from the bombs is bright enough to give a pilot flash blindness, ruin his dark adaptation and permanently damage the retina by burning a hole in it. Rather than simulate, the experts used rabbits in actual field conditions. During the 1950s rabbits were taken aloft in airplanes, harnessed to the windows and forced to look out at atmospheric tests. But Colonel Huycke says: "The animals would blink just as the bomb was going off, ruining the entire experiment. Now, when you pay a lot ' of money for a project like that you hate to see the dumb animals mess it up. So the problem was solved in successive experiments by sewing the rabbits' eyelids open so they would have to look out the plane at the blast. But then we found out that pink rabbit eyes tend to reflect more light than human eyes normally would."

Since 1960 D.N.A. has funded three studies that use human volunteers to help the Pentagon understand the effects of nuclear warfare. The old rabbit tests have been replaced by an optical study at the Medical College of Virginia in Richmond at a cost of 30,000 dollars a year. Colonel Huycke says essentially what they have done is to find people "about to undergo enucleation [removal of the eye for cancer] and explain to them the pressing need for realistic evaluation of the retinal-burn hazard from nuclear weapons and laser sources. We ask them if they would allow us to painlessly burn their eyes just before surgery. A zeon strobe light is used to burn the retina in 20 or 25 places with varying degrees of light. After the eye is removed, the scientists examine the retina with a microscope to see the damage done by the light beam. This has given us a great deal of information about the flashburn problem."

Another experiment at Walter Reed Army Medical Center calculates the effects of massive doses of radiation absorbed in combat. This study, funded at 50,000 dollars a year, uses patients who are undergoing radiation therapy to arrest brain tumors. In this established form of treatment intense doses of radiation are focused on the brain. After irradiation, patients are subjected to special psychological tests to find out how their minds have been affected. Eleven other subjects in this Reed experiment have undergone spinal irradiation. The scientists study these patients to see if radiation affects their ability to use the fine muscles. Colonel Huycke says this work is finding out "if radiation affects the nerves in the spinal cord and the spinal muscles. Then experiments are conducted to see if the radiation exposure has affected the patient's grip or sense of touch. We see if he can feel the difference between a nickel and a dime, that sort of thing."

The most comprehensive of these D.N.A. studies on radiation effects is conducted at the University of Cincinnati College of Medicine under the leadership of one of the nation's most prominent radiologists, Eugene L. Saenger. Dr. Saenger is founder of the University of Cincinnati's radioactive isotope laboratory and the school's center for nuclear medicine. He has lectured and published widely on such matters as thyroid cancer, the acute radiation syndrome and metabolic change caused by radiation. Dr. Saenger also sits on the prestigious National Council on Radiological Protection, which advises the federal government on radiation-exposure standards.

The Cincinnati physician has been one of the leading defenders of the nation's current radiation-protection standards against a growing number of critics who charge they are causing excess cancers. Dr. Karl Z. Morgan, of the A.E.C.'s Oak Ridge Laboratory, for example, argues that diagnostic X rays are causing between 3,500 and 29,000 extra deaths a year. And Drs. John Gofman and Arthur R. Tamplin have argued that allowable radiation-exposure standards could cause an excess 32,000 cancers annually.

Dr. Saenger disagrees with these arguments and believes any change in the standards could be a drastic setback for nuclear medicine and the nation. In a statement submitted to the Joint Committee on Atomic Energy in January 1970, Dr. Saenger pointed out that, if current trends continue, soon "any part of the field of nuclear medicine should be as good or better an investment than IBM or Coca-Cola from the time they were founded."

Of course, Dr. Saenger went on to say that he was much more concerned with the way nuclear medicine was helping to cure disease and in that regard "what is good from radiation is good for the country." For these reasons he concluded that the nation's current radiation-exposure standards are safe and "should be altered only when new human data indicate that such changes are required."

Getting that human data is very difficult. Most of the serious studies on the effects of heavy doses of radiation in this country have been performed on laboratory animals. Saenger says that "extrapolation of results from laboratory animals to man can be fraught with error." Even the studies at Walter Reed have their limitations, because they focus the radiation on a small part of the body. The only way to get really good human data is to irradiate the whole body or a good portion of it, as is done with laboratory animals. This way one can study the acute radiation syndrome in humans.

One of the biggest studies in this field is run by Dr. Saenger at the University of Cincinnati with funding from the D.N.A. This study has been going on since February 1960 and has cost D.N.A. over $500,000. In fiscal 1971 it was funded at 93,000 dollars. In these D.N.A. studies, Dr. Saenger and his team take victims of inoperable cancer and expose them to "total-body and partial-body [generally radiation of the upper or lower body] radiation so as to obtain a better understanding of these acute and subacute effects in human beings. This information is necessary to provide knowledge of combat effectiveness of troops and to develop more suitable methods of diagnosis, prognosis, prophylaxis, and treatment of radiation injuries. It is our belief that information concerning radiation effects in the human being can be determined as well or better in these subjects as in the laboratory animal even though the characteristic of the cancer [in the patient] must be kept in mind in the evaluation of the data."

In the first ten years of the experiments 91 patients were exposed to the radiation, and by the fall of 1970 some 64 had been fully evaluated. Careful records on their medical and psychological response to the radiation dose were kept as an aid to help D.N.A. figure out how much radiation troops can take in combat and continue to fight effectively. Saenger has concluded that troops can take up to 200 rads and still keep fighting. But a second dose of 200 rads or more would render many soldiers "combat ineffective immediately."

Dr. Saenger's D.N.A. reports indicate that when a patient is selected for this project, "there is no discussion of possible subjective reactions resulting from the treatment. Other physicians, nurses, technicians and ward personnel are instructed not to discuss symptoms or reactions with the patient." The patient must sign a release signifying that the "nature and purpose of this therapy, possible alternative methods of treatment, the risks involved, the possibility of complications and prognosis have been fully explained to me. The special study and research nature of this treatment has been discussed with me and is understood by me." But Dr. Saenger says he is "not sure whether or not patients are actually told that the research is being done for D.N.A."

Dr. Saenger does, however, make certain to tell his patients that he hopes the whole body radiation exposure they are receiving will cure or at least allieviate their cancer. He administers doses up to 200 rads. The Atomic Energy Commission says that if a healthy person were to receive this much radiation he might develop "radiation illness. . . . Whole body irradiation (experimental animals and human experience) has been shown to result in such chronic effects as early aging, cancer and life shortening." Dr. Saenger says that if a healthy individual is exposed to 300 rads he has about a 50-percent chance of survival.

However humans can survive much higher radiation doses if they are focused on a small area. In fact a common form of cancer therapy is to focus 5,000 to 7,000 rads directly on a tumor. This form of treatment can arrest the tumor. The high doses are used because a few hundred rads focused on a tumor probably would not be able to arrest all the cancer cells. Five thousand to 7,000 rads might be able to do it. Dr. Saenger's patients are all victims of incurable tumors and his technique involves exposing them to as much as 200 rads of whole body radiation in an attempt to allieviate the cancer. Is his D.N.A. research saving lives? A review of Dr. Saenger's reports to D.N.A. between February 1960 and October 1970 indicates that 53 of his 91 cancer patients have died. Among one group of 37 patients exposed to total body radiation, the median survival time was 200 days. In a 1967 speech in Berkeley, California, Dr. Saenger said that "the effect of radiation on lethality . . . has been difficult to interpret," in a group of selected patients. Much of the difficulty is Dr. Saenger's inability to set up a control group of cancer patients to compare against those getting his whole body radiation exposure: "It would be . . . difficult to obtain concurrent patients with neoplasms [tumors] similar in extent and pathological type," he explained in his Berkeley speech.

There are some experts who disagree with this contention. One is Dr. John Gofman of the A.E.C.'s Lawrence Radiation Laboratory at Livermore, California: "Conventional radiation therapy to solid tumors is generally in the neighborhood of 5,000 to 7,000 rads. The reason for this dose is to make sure the probability of killing the cancer is high. It is difficult to see how a low dose could have a high probability of killing cancer cells in small nests around the body. What good does it do to give a small dose of a few hundred rads that might kill 50 percent of the cells when the remaining cells will continue to multiply?" Dr. Gofman, who has done a considerable amount of cancer research himself, suggests that: "In view of this uncertainty, plus the fact that we know whole body radiation of a few hundred rads can be very dangerous, it seems hard to understand why there is no control group. There are hundreds of thousands of cancer patients in America, certainly there ought to be enough around to provide Dr. Saenger with a suitable control group. Without the control there is no definitive way to understand if the patients have truly benefited from this whole body treatment in terms of feeling or extension of life. Certainly other cancer studies use control groups. One wonders why Saenger's study ostensibly aimed toward alleviation of cancer is so inadequate."

Dr. Saenger, however, believes that the D.N.A. studies are doing much to help protect his countrymen. He says "the most important field of investigation today is that of attempting to understand and mitigate the possible effects of nuclear warfare upon human beings. I'm a person who takes the defense of our country very seriously. I think it is important to find out the kind of things we are learning in this study." The patients' contribution to data usually begins soon after irradiation. Dr. Saenger's team watches to see if the radiation causes vomiting. If so, the experts must note how long the nausea lasts. This sort of information is very important to D.N.A. because it allows them to figure out how long troops will be "combat ineffective" after receiving varying degrees of radiation.

In their reports to D.N.A. the Cincinnati group provides brief summaries on each patient. For example, in their October

1970 report Dr. Saenger's group wrote: "A ten-year-old Caucasian female was admitted to Children's Hospital on February 17, 1969, for whole-body irradiation and evaluation of her previously diagnosed Ewing's sarcoma. . . . She was treated on February 17, 1969, with 200-rad midline absorbed tissue dose of total-body irradiation. Nausea and vomiting occurred within sixty minutes; however, after eleven hours these symptoms subsided. . . . The patient remains in good condition 195 days post TBR [total body radiation]."

Another patient was a 49-year-old Black female who was given a "150 rad midline absorbed tissue dose [of] total body radiation." She "experienced nausea, vomiting, and anorexia until early afternoon of the day of treatment." Nineteen days later she was very short of breath and coughing frequently. Her white blood count and platelet count dropped, she rapidly deteriorated and died 30 days post total body radiation.

Generally the team has found that "the incidence of prodromal nausea, vomiting, and anorexia [loss of appetite] rose with increasing dose in patients receiving TBR, being far more frequent above 125 rad." A number of standard psychological tests have also been administered to measure cognitive impairment, depression, verbal behavior and mood after the radiation. Dr. Saenger says: "It has been difficult to evaluate these studies in part because of the low educational levels and intelligence quotients of these patients," who are usually elderly general-hospital patients.

Another problem encountered in administering the psychological tests is nausea. In one test a Saenger team trying to evaluate the verbal behavior of patients following irradiation reported that "nausea intervened and they [the patients] were not able to accomplish the verbal behavior task."

The group has been also somewhat limited in its study of physical performance following irradiation. One report notes that "the structure of our studies at present does not lend itself well to investigation of physical decrements since our patients are old, ill, and may well have unknown metastases [malignant tumors]. Treadmill tests and similar ones which place a load on work capacity are not being pursued at this time."

The patients also have been broken down into groups of long-term survivors, who lived more than 100 days after treatment, and short-term survivors, who lived less than 100 days after treatment. The experts found, on the average, short-term survivors seemed considerably more depressed and less hopeful than the long-term survivors.

Dr. Saenger says that besides helping his patients and D.N.A., his work has contributed to a wide variety of biochemical, immunological and chromosomal studies relating to radiation. He is proud of his project and happy to talk about it. D.N.A. is also proud of the work but is not happy to talk about it. Colonel Huycke says: "I think you can appreciate the situation—a family comes, let's say, from the hills of Kentucky. 'My child has tumor of the kidney.' The doctor sees that this is bad, probably the child is going to die. Now Dr. Saenger is going to see if he can arrest it or stop it with his treatment. First of all, the family, the patient, all consent to have the treatment. This is Dr. Saenger's recommendation: 'I think I can help you, here's what I hope to do.' So he says, 'Can we do some of this psychological testing which you read for us, before and after like this? We won't harm you.' Whether these patients know or care that psychological testing is being done, at least partly for the Defense Nuclear Agency, I don't know. But I can well appreciate that some sad families who lost a child in spite of the treatment could be misled to think, 'My child was used for the bomb people.' That could be a heartbreak to that family, and a needless one, because D.N.A.'s interest had nothing to do with the application of the very best known medical treatment. The child is treated medically by the University of Cincinnati, by a procedure thought up by the professor of radiology, and the treatment is cleared by them. This is of concern to me, dealing with patients. If it comes out in the paper little Jimmie Jones was sick and dying and suddenly he is now used for the bomb . . ."

Dr. Saenger, too, wants his project work to be seen in the proper light. He believes the research is leading to better cancer therapy and helping protect the nation. Dr. Saenger is a bit impatient with people who want to get in the way of nuclear research.

In his January 1970 statement to the J.C.A.E., he issued a ringing defense of existing federal radiation-exposure standards and then turned to another vital matter, "the support of radiology by the federal government." He voiced concern that federal support of scientific research was falling off generally and said that Pentagon support of pertinent research on effects of nuclear weapons is tending "to become smaller in spite of the fact that the problem of treatment of the acute radiation syndrome and consequences of high-dose fallout remain unresolved. The responsibility of continuing the search for better therapy for these high-dose injuries from radiation must be a major concern of physicians and especially radiologists. The threat of this kind of injury is as great in my opinion as the actuality of problems of cancer and far more study of these conditions is required. . . . It is essential that we press every effort to indicate to the persons responsible for these programs the concern which we have not only for research . . . but also for provision of adequate training to career men in the several services and universities so that we have a highly trained and highly skilled pool of scientifically qualified men who will be available at a moment's notice should they be needed in case of nuclear warfare or other catastrophe."

CHAPTER SEVEN

POSTATTACK

Most Americans do not look forward to life after nuclear war. But the Pentagon's Office of Civil Defense says that is because they do not realize "postattack" society will offer certain advantages over preattack society. After the fallout clears, rent, taxes and consumer debts may all be canceled. Abandonment of old people, chronic invalids and the insane will lighten the welfare load. Per capita wealth will increase and it seems likely that everyone will get a promotion. No one will starve because there will be plenty of potato chips to go around.

Over the past decade the O.C.D. and the A.E.C. have spent over 86 million dollars to tell us about the good side of nuclear war. By underestimating the size of nuclear attacks, ignoring the realities of fallout and the genetic effects of radiation, the postattack researchers in the universities and think-tanks insist that postattack society can be fun.

So the enemy penetrates our defense system. That does not mean the world has come to an end. Do not panic about being packed into a community fallout shelter. Actually the overcrowding "is effective in reducing fatalities to occupants" provided "overheating is not a serious problem." Just be sure to bring along your sleeping pills and Bible, says the O.C.D. Before you know it, you will be ready for evacuation to the country. For example, Los Angeles residents can look forward to relocation in the desert—a delightful change of pace as long as you remember to bring along your room air conditioner. Others will be moved to mountain caverns, a good place to be as long as you bring your down parka. And forget those silly fears about radiation sickness. The civil-defense experts say radiation "is not contagious or infectious and one person cannot catch it from another." Yes, you will have a fine time in the great postattack society where people will be forever willing to sacrifice for the good of one another.

The scores of studies on postattack plagues, floods, food supplies, water supplies, banking, transportation, education, government and the rest of contemporary society share a common optimism that serves a dual function, First, they keep the government happy by advancing the fiction that nuclear war is survivable, so generals and politicians can play with their "nuclear option." Second, they keep the postattack researcher employed. Were he to use valid scenarios of all-out war, instead of token nuclear attacks, there would be virtually nothing left to evaluate. But, by claiming that nuclear war is survivable, he validates the need for his own work and opens the way to further research that keeps him on the public tit.

Thus a study of postattack food supplies in San Jose, California, naturally leads to similar studies in other cities around the country. Another variant is changing the size of the theoretical attack. What would happen in a one-, ten-, and 100-megaton attack? Of course, even in the worst attacks the experts must remain optimistic about survival prospects: "I can write you any kind of nuclear-war scenario you want," says Dr. H. H. Mitchell of the Rand Corporation. "But no matter how bad the war is, man is going to survive. Even if a billion people are killed, you still will have a couple billion left. On the biological time scale, nuclear war will not have any effect on the species. Sure, I think it is total insanity to have nuclear weapons. But I think it compounds the insanity not to have civil-defense programs to figure out what we should do after a nuclear war."

Dr. Mitchell and the other postattack researchers for the O.C.D. and A.E.C. stay sane by writing reports that make Armageddon palatable. Lengthy analysis frequently leads to simplistic conclusions. Thus a nuclear weapon striking an atomic power plant is considered no hazard because "most of the radioactivity released from the core [of the reactor] should be deposited in the area already damaged by nuclear-weapons effects and cause no additional casualties." Likewise Human Sciences Research, Inc., concludes that the news media should have little trouble operating with a skeleton staff of survivors when the war is over:

"A typical newspaper of 35 pages contains less than three pages of essential news . . . The news media thus should be able to carry out their tasks under . . . emergency conditions because their task can be reduced and it is possible for fewer men to duplicate the services that are often done by many. . . . Again for radio stations, probably fewer than 25 percent of the employees, including all those associated with broadcasting, are necessary for the transmission of news and instructions."

The experts who work in this carnivorous never-never land find their research matter in unusual places. Thus the Stanford Research Institute publishes a 137-page report suggesting how Hitler's wartime industrial controls could be useful in postattack society. Hints are taken from the testimony of convicted Nazi war criminals at the Nuremburg trials. The author says he is only being practical: "For reasons of taste . . . contemporary historians have neglected the recent economic history of Germany, preferring to chronicle the sorry record of Nazi horrors. The report deliberately ignores this fact of German wartime experience."

At the Rand Corporation scientists justify their imaginative postwar ideas by claiming they are telling "what is likely to be done rather than what should be done" after the bomb falls. Under this cover Rand demographer Ira S. Lowry talks about how to rebuild society in an A.E.C. study on *The Post-Attack Population of the U. S.:*

> Depending on the international environment, public priorities might go either to restoring the nation's military strength or to rebuilding the industrial plant. Whichever the goal, the rele-

vant view of the nation's population is as both resource and burden. . . . Survivors . . . in their productive years—roughly 15
to 64 by present standards—would clearly be the most valuable
segment of the post-attack population. They would have to be
kept in good health and encouraged to produce their utmost, to
go where they were needed, to transfer their skills from frivolous
to serious occupations. Providing them with bare subsistence con-
sistent with health might not be enough to motivate them as producers; individually and collectively, the labor force would be in
a strong position to exact preferential treatment at the hands of
the government. Furthermore it would be impossible to limit
preferential treatment to labor-force members alone, for the
working members of society would insist on transferring some
part of their personal advantages to members of their families
who were not directly contributing to output.

Policymakers would presumably have to draw the line
somewhere, however, in making such concessions, and those most
likely to suffer are people with little or no productive potential:
old people, chronic invalids, and the insane. Old people suffer the
special disadvantage of being easily identified as a group and
therefore subject to categorical treatment. In the short run, of
course, neither extreme of the age distribution would have value
as a source of manpower, but children at least are tomorrow's
workers. On the other hand, not even a long-run view bestows
value as a resource on the elderly members of society. In a liter-
ate community, the elderly do not even serve their prehistoric
function as repositories of traditional wisdom. Since the amount
of care and attention necessary to sustain life increases with age,
this drain on national resources could significantly affect recovery
planning. In this sense at least a community under stress would
be better off without its old and feeble members.

And just how would we go about this? Well, Mr. Lowry
thinks:

The easiest way to implement a morally repugnant but so-
cially beneficial policy is by inaction. Under stress, the managers
of post-attack society would most likely resolve their problem by
failing to make any special provision for the special needs of the
elderly, the insane, and the chronically ill. Instead of Medicare
for persons over 65, for example, we might have Medicare for
persons under 15. Instead of pensions, we might have family al-
lowances. To be sure, the government would not be able—nor
would it be likely to try—to prevent the relatives and friends of

old people from helping them, but overall the share of the elderly in the national product would certainly drop.

Public policy toward surviving children would probably be more generous. The nearer these are to labor-force age, the greater their present value as producers, and the less costly it would be to protect them either as clients or as social capital. But one can imagine public policy toward maternity passing through two phases. In the immediate post-attack period, the primary goal being to maximize the economic surplus, children would have no short-run value. Since it is easier to reject public responsibility for the individual welfare of the unborn than of persons already living, an antinatal policy would be the most plausible way to reduce the short-run dependency rate and free women for the labor-force participation. . . . As recovery got under way, a pronatal policy would probably replace the antinatal.

Lowry realizes, of course, that many people would want to flee from this sort of postattack society: "Assuming that other parts of the world were in better shape, emigration would offer a serious challenge to government authority. For individuals and family groups, beginning over again in South America might be a much more attractive prospect than an austere existence in a radio-active United States." The Rand expert worries, though, that such a mass emigration would deprive the United States of imaginative citizens and suggests that emigration be prevented through a flat ban or moral suasion. One incentive to keep people at home is that "the casualty rate would be higher among the organizational élite, [so] it might be possible to give nearly everyone a promotion."

Rand's Dr. Mitchell seconds Lowry's contention that the post-attack employment picture would be solid: "After the plague wiped out 25 percent of the population in Europe, the survivors had a good time. There was a severe labor shortage and the peasants who survived found themselves in demand for every sort of work. Well, it's the same thing in postattack society. We will need more of everything from typists to Negro maids. Of course, we joke about this, but humor is just a safety valve to stop us from going crazy in this business. It's like the doctor telling a dirty joke in the autopsy room."

New job opportunities are only one of the special benefits

accruing to the survivors. An Institute for Defense Analysis study shows that a nuclear attack will actually give everyone in Houston more property. The study, called *The Effects of Nuclear Weapons on a Single City,* says: "In a macabre sense the surviving population would be individually wealthier than before the attack. For a single 10-megaton weapon, surviving property value per capita nearly doubles from a preattack value of about $9,000 to slightly more than $16,000 and as the weight of the attack increases the greater the per capita gain in 'wealth' of the survivors. For a 100-megaton surface burst the surviving population is nearly four times wealthier than pre-attack ($34,000)."

Another cold-blooded analysis, by Human Sciences Research, Inc., suggests the tax advantages of nuclear war. It points out that individual income taxes may not be assessed because they "would be most difficult to collect." It also recommends a moratorium on consumer debts and rental payments, but warns the impact of these actions will vary: "A moratorium on consumer debts would affect a large proportion of survivors. A moratorium on rent payments, on the other hand, would be ineffective to the extent that rented housing had been destroyed."

Another section of this report wonders if nuclear devastation might persuade individuals to eschew free enterprise and share the wealth. The researchers say that one of the "therapeutic effects of disaster" is that it produces "communities of sufferers exerting common efforts to meet the perceived threat." Could not this community spirit destroy the capitalist spirit and foster socialism? Never, say University of Tennessee professors D. A. Patterson and J. R. Moore in *Planning for Economic Recovery from Thermonuclear Attack.* "Confiscation of . . . 'excess' income and wealth . . . is not generally assumed to be feasible because (a) it contradicts flagrantly our traditional ideology concerning wealth and income; (b) it would probably have severe disincentive effects, contributing to more waste than it would alleviate; (c) it would be very difficult to administer."

The fate of free enterprise is a prime concern of all postattack research. A broad Stanford Research Institute study is looking at postattack food availability in five American cities: San

Jose, California; Albuquerque, New Mexico; New Orleans, Louisiana; Providence, Rhode Island; and Detroit, Michigan. The scientists conduct simulated attacks and then calculate the fate of every food processor in town. For example, the nuclear attack on San Jose destroys 20 percent of the stocks at the Jack Frost Creamery, 50 percent of the inventory at Stempel Quality Donut Shop and the Sunsweet Prune cannery, and 70 percent of the Granny Goose potato chip factory. In Albuquerque, Thelma Lu's Candies burns down and the New Mexico Dog Food Company loses half its stocks; Albuquerque Cackleberries loses all its eggs.

These S.R.I. studies show survivors will initially experience certain privations in postattack society. The Albuquerque report says that during the first month after nuclear war "survivors may anticipate severe shortages of every commodity except potatoes." Fluid milk will be the scarcest item because of "depletion of local dairy herds due to radiation sickness" and contamination of the milk produced by surviving cows. The milk will be usable only when put into a processed form like cheese and aged so that its radioactivity can decay to safe levels. Although meat, eggs, vegetables and other staples will be available, blast damage should temporarily inhibit their transport to market. This will also be a bad time for a Coke or other carbonated beverage because only 39 percent of the Albuquerque soft-drink bottling industry is projected to survive the nuclear attack. Both the Coca-Cola and Canada Dry bottling companies are a total loss. Pepsi-Cola, Royal Crown and 7-Up bottlers take moderate to heavy blast damage but are expected to regain production capacity within a couple of months. Unfortunately bottling at these three firms could be held up by a severe sugar shortage that may also hurt the makers of "bakery products, sweetened condensed milk, canned fruits, jams and jellies, and confectionery products."

But, despite these problems, no one will starve. One "particularly valuable post-attack crop"—the potato—should make it. "The survival of much of the national harvest coupled with the immediate availability of the local crop guarantees that Albuquerque survivors will not lack potatoes at any time during the first post attack year. . . . Although no processing is necessary in the case of the potato . . . it is worth noting that 76.4 percent of Berna-lillo County [metropolitan Albuquerque] pre-attack potato proc-essing potential is expected to survive the attack. This figure re-flects the survival of the plant and management of three local potato chip manufacturers capable of processing roughly 5.8 mil-lion pounds of potatoes in the first post-attack year. This process-ing capability would have the effect of offering a certain dietary variety to local survivors who will be heavily dependent on pota-toes for sustenance in the early post-attack months."

Some scientists also believe certain radioactive foods could be edible. Former A.E.C. Commissioner Willard Libby says that "strontium-contaminated land could still be used to produce corn or other fodder for cows and pigs to produce beef and pork. This flesh probably would be safe to eat. And beef cattle could graze on these lands. . . . Other land lightly dusted—since it was far-ther from the bombed area—could be used to grow food for hu-mans, although it might contain some strontium and cesium. There would be a better chance of growing safe crops for human consumption in high-calcium soils, because calcium competes with strontium to enter the crops."

Some of the scientists who make these macabre predictions occasionally concede the obvious: they are working in a fantasy land appropriate only for science-fiction late shows. In conducting its so-called BRISK/FRISK simulated attack, the Institute for Defense Analysis mentions that "any estimate of the number of fatalities in a future nuclear attack cannot avoid being vulnerable to many possible sources of error such as . . . magnitude, . . . timing, and location of the attack." The scientists point out there are "at least 18 additional sources of error cited in this study that have not been considered. In order to maintain perspective, it should be noted that the variability of nature (i.e., changes in wind patterns) can produce changes in fatality estimates."

And the same I.D.A. study that predicts nuclear war will in-crease Houston per capita wealth cautions: "Any joy among the surviving population may be quite short-lived; none of these gross estimates of the effects of nuclear attack indicates whether or not the immediate metropolitan area is viable, either by itself or with the assistance of the rest of the country."

This logic would seem obvious to anyone past the eighth grade, but it seems to have eluded the postattack researchers in their lust for loot. All they have returned for federal millions is an object lesson in how to warp social science to support any dictum. Little if any of what they predict can be trusted; postattack life cannot be planned like the weekly shopping list. But if the bomb does fall, let us hope that one, just one, of their multitudinous predictions is borne out. That prophecy comes from the HRB-Singer Company, which writes in its *Summary of Social Institutions and Thermonuclear War* that nuclear attack would "cause a high reduction in the research capability of the higher education system as a whole." Some might call it divine retribution.

CHAPTER EIGHT

OCCUPATIONAL HEALTH

While leaders of nuclear government believe in spending tens of millions to prepare America for postattack society, very little is spent to protect preattack society. The men who work in the uranium mines, the plutonium fabrication plants and test ranges, the people who live near these nuclear zones are kept in continual ignorance of radiation hazards. The government atomic-energy officials believe it is better this way. They see no reason for the public to worry about this nuclear threat inside America. When a television reporter asks the chairman of the Joint Committee on Atomic Energy if the public knows "enough about radiation," the legislator replies: "No and it never will, because it's too complicated a matter. They don't know as much as they should know about cancer or about the handling of nitroglycerin or sulfuric acid, either, but that doesn't mean that precautions aren't being taken by those who do know to protect the person who does not know."

Such bland reassurances have always been uttered by the men who have led the atomic-energy industry. Those who raise doubts about the safety of the weapons business are derided as sensationalists or worrywarts. But the same nuclear scientists who claim to be protecting the workers and the public have often failed to protect themselves. The very men who have dumped debris on hapless natives because they could not forecast the wind, insist they know what they are doing. Neighbors of nuclear-weapons facilities are constantly reassured all is perfectly safe. And every time a new employee goes to work in one of these installations he can count on being told he is safer on the job than he is at the nearest highway intersection. No one has recorded the exact source of this oft-told certitude, but it may well emanate from the career of Pierre Curie, who discovered radium with his wife, Marie. It seems that Pierre was anxious to assess the biological effect of this mysterious new substance. Rather than search far afield for a guinea pig, Pierre chose to expose his own arm to a radium source for ten hours. His skin began to blush immediately, then turned bright red, formed scabs and finally a wound that was dressed in bandages. Some 42 days after exposure the epidermis began to form on the edge, working toward the center, and on the fifty-second day the wound turned gray, indicating deeper mortification.

Pierre Curie died a short time later, not from the radiation but from injuries sustained when being run down by a carriage. In this sense, perhaps the A.E.C. is right when it says that one is safer in a nuclear laboratory than out on the highway. But the fate of Pierre's wife, daughter Irène and son-in-law Frédéric suggest nuclear work has its dangers, too. All three died from diseases induced through working with radioactive materials.

In fact, during the first two to three decades following the discovery of X rays, about two pounds of radium were extracted from the earth and abused in ways that killed at least 100 people. The occupational overexposures began soon after Wilhelm Roentgen discovered X rays in 1895. One of the first to learn about radiation hazard was Henry Bequerel, who proved that uranium salts give off penetrating rays. Bequerel took a small glass vial of radium and carried it in his pocket for several days until he burned himself. Thomas Edison was very enthusiastic about X rays but decided to quit using them after one of his assistants died from a radiation overdose. Promoters who tried to use X rays for hair removal ended up burning patients' arms, necessitating amputations. In 1924 America was mortified by exposure of a classic case of radium poisoning that eventually took the lives of about 40 radium-dial painters at a New Jersey watch factory. The victims were young women who had been pointing brushes with their tongues and, of course, ingesting fatal doses of radium. Even many of the pioneer radiologists trying to help patients ended up killing themselves with overexposures.

The scientists who developed the bomb technology were also careless. The University of California Radiation Laboratory (now the Lawrence Radiation Laboratory) was plagued by frightful ignorance of radiation hazards in the early days. In 1935 physician John Lawrence paid a visit to his brother Ernest, who directed the burgeoning laboratory on the Berkeley campus. John was shocked to learn that the physicists had almost no idea of radiation's dangers. When he tried to warn them, they only joked. Ernest, who would go on to win the Nobel prize for his pioneering nuclear physics, was so anxious to demonstrate the strange nature of radiation that he staged public showings at a Berkeley auditorium. At one performance he uncorked a bottle of sodium 24, one of his newest concoctions, with a radioactive half-life of 15 hours. The sample was so hot that it overloaded a Geiger counter, so Lawrence called his fellow scientist J. Robert Oppenheimer out of the audience, had him place a hand around the Geiger counter and drink a glass of water containing some of the sodium. Fifty seconds later the Geiger counter clattered away. Lawrence had proved that the radioactive material reached the bloodstream in just 50 seconds.

Although Oppenheimer was not harmed, the experiment was nonetheless a foolish bit of showmanship. The leaders of the nuclear research at Berkeley in those days never seemed to be concerned about basic safety precautions. Scientists working at the Crocker cyclotron would come back to the chemistry department with laboratory coats so radioactive that Geiger counters started clattering. But experts were only worried about their precious experiments being thrown off by this extra radiation. They never stopped to think the contamination might also endanger their peers. After all, the young men who joined the Berkeley plutonium project in those days were getting a chance to work with the masters, so why shouldn't they accept a few risks?

For example, in 1941, after chemist Glenn Seaborg and his young graduate student John Gofman co-discovered uranium 233, Gofman was assigned to demonstrate that uranium 233 was fissionable with neutrons. Such evidence would open up the world's thorium supply as a vast new source of atomic energy. Gofman was to bombard the virgin isotope with a one-gram radium-beryllium neutron source. A gram of radium-beryllium is deadly stuff moved about inside lead containers. To protect himself, Gofman went to work building a small conveyor that would transport the hot neutron source up to the uranium 233 by remote control. But Dr. Seaborg was impatient. One day he dropped by and chided Gofman for being overly concerned with safety. "The war will be over before you get any [fission] measurements this way," he said. So Dr. Seaborg came up with a better idea. Gofman remembers being instructed to tie a rope to the radium-beryllium source and to connect it to a big stick. Like a fisherman, he could cast the hot neutron source across the room to the uranium 233, where the fission test could be conducted. Seaborg left the room and Gofman did precisely what he was told. The experiment succeeded. Uranium 233 was fissionable. Seaborg went on to win the Nobel prize and become chairman of the A.E.C.; Gofman received a disastrous overdose of radiation, at least 100 times the permissible exposure level. So far, Gofman has fortunately experienced no ill effects from the overexposure.

When the plutonium project became part of the Manhattan Project in 1943, the government did set up safety patrols. But they were hardly adequate. Dr. Gofman remembers that "to produce the first milligram of plutonium at Berkeley we went to the Berkeley cyclotron and bombarded a ton of uranyl nitrate with neutrons for a couple months. Then it was brought over to the chemistry department and dissolved in four big vats of dilute acid to separate away the uranium and concentrate the plutonium. Despite some crude lead shielding, everyone in the room was getting bombarded with a couple of rads a day. By today's standards we would have only been allowed to work in such a hot room for a few days, but everyone went on with this business for weeks. When the Manhattan Project safety people came in to inspect, they weren't worried about the overexposure. Their only fear was our practice of stacking cardboard uranyl-nitrate shipping containers in one corner of the room. They said the boxes might fall over and hit someone."

Even Enrico Fermi's team, at the University of Chicago, had some contamination problems. One of Fermi's young aides was Harold Agnew, now director of the Los Alamos Scientific Laboratory. While the experts were setting up the pile beneath the university's football stadium, Agnew was given the job of transferring hot radium-beryllium sources for use in albedo experiments. None of the nuclear experts realized how dangerous frequent handling of these sources could be until Agnew went to the Indiana Dunes at Lake Michigan for a holiday in June 1942. The sunlight's infrared rays reacted with the gamma and neutron exposure Agnew had received from the radioactive source. His skin turned bright red, began swelling up and blisters began appearing. Agnew was ill for several weeks and recalls looking somewhat like the "Michelin Man," the bloated giant used for advertising the French tires. After Agnew recovered, the Chicago pile leaders decided he would no longer work with hot sources. He was transferred to "cold" duties.

Radiological safety procedures were, to the very end of the war, most primitive. When the *Enola Gay* took off from Tinian to bomb Hiroshima, the experts were, of course, concerned that the plane might crash and detonate Little Boy. So a team of experts under the leadership of Raemer E. Schreiber were posted on a hill two miles from the runway and prepared to cordon off the area in the event of a crash. Schreiber, who is now an associate director of the Los Alamos laboratory, "won't say whether or not we really knew what we were doing."

Even Enrico Fermi, who died of cancer in 1954 at the age of fifty-three (A.E.C. Chairman Louis Strauss would go to Fermi's deathbed and give him a medal, 25,000 dollars and news that the agency was establishing an award in his name for outstanding scientists), could not stomach some of the recklessness in the Manhattan Project. One Fermi crew at Los Alamos worked in a small building shared by a macabre thirty-three-year-old physicist named Louis Slotin. Slotin and his associates performed the vital, and terribly dangerous, critical-assembly tests to position the nuclear components at the precise distance necessary to set off a chain reaction and nuclear blast. These tests must be made for each new weapon design. Today they are performed remotely at complex "critical-assembly machines" by operators located a quarter of a mile away. In those days Slotin and his team actually pushed the hemispherical nuclear components together with a screwdriver and then measured radiation with a Geiger counter and a neutron monitor. The pieces were shoved close enough together to begin a chain reaction. But they were always pulled apart before the material became overcritical, because this would easily deliver a fatal dose of radiation to the scientists. Fermi was so dismayed by the young man's relish for this task ("tickling the dragon's tail," Slotin called it) that he would take his own crew hiking in the Sangre de Cristo Mountains each time Slotin conducted one of his assemblies.

Slotin took his dangerous job very seriously. Indeed, he was depressed for weeks after the Japanese nuclear bombings, because authorities had refused to let him accompany his bombs to their targets, as an observer. Slotin was given a vacation to sulk and his chief assistant, Harry Daghlian, went to work on the criticality experiments necessary to build new atomic bombs. Daghlian promptly overexposed himself in a criticality accident and Slotin returned to stand vigil at his friend's bedside during the month he lay dying.

Daghlian's death shocked the Los Alamos community and prompted the experts to design a simple spring-actuated safety device that would push the nuclear components apart if they got too close together in a critical-assembly test. But Slotin insisted on continuing to conduct the critical-assembly tests by hand, pushing the pieces together with his screwdriver. He claimed a "feeling for the experiment" that made them safe.

Slotin went on conducting his critical-assembly tests during the fall and winter of 1945–46 as he had done for the previous two years. Finally, in the spring, a plan was underway to shift the criticality tests to a new, remote-control facility. Slotin's era at Los Alamos was ending and he was about to get a special bonus, a free trip to Bikini to watch the Able atmospheric-test shot. Then he would probably return to university life. With a tinge of nostalgia Slotin performed his critical-assembly test one last time, on May 21, 1946, for the edification of his successor, Al Graves, and six other men who chanced to be in the room. Slotin, who had conducted this test 40 times, approached this final exercise with his usual confidence. The slim, serious scientist pushed the pieces toward one another as usual but suddenly he slipped and the room filled with a blue ionization glow. The Geiger counter chattered, Slotin lunged forward and flung the hemispheres apart while one of the men yelled, "Let's get the hell out of here!" Seven men charged out of the room, their lives saved by Slotin, who knew instantly that he had taken a fatal dose of radiation. His first concern was Al Graves, who had been at his shoulder. Would he survive? He put the computation to Graves' wife, Elizabeth, without telling her what had happened. Mrs. Graves believed herself a stoic; she once dismissed Hiroshima as nothing worse than napalm. But she froze when she learned who the subject of her calculation was. Al Graves survived with cataracts and went on to direct nuclear tests in the Pacific. The other six men survived, too. But Slotin had taken about 880 rads, the equivalent of being exposed to an atomic bomb at a distance of 4,800 feet. During the first 12 hours after his exposure Slotin vomited repeatedly. His hands turned red, swelled and became bluish at the nails. His arms were packed in ice to keep the swelling down and the abdomen became red and tender. Ten doctors were brought in to consult. General Groves cheered Slotin with a letter and flew the scientist's parents in from Manitoba on an Army charter plane. Slotin's white blood count dropped rapidly; his pulse rose while his weight dropped and his mind began to fail. He sank into a coma; on May 30, 1946, nine days after the experiment, he died. His funeral drew scientists from across the nation, and his parents permitted an autopsy so that Louis Slotin's tragedy could benefit the cause of science.

Tragic though Slotin's death was, at least the A.E.C. dignified his career by conceding that radiation killed him. Only two other men have been so honored (Harry Daghlian and a Los Alamos employee killed in a 1958 radiation accident). The A.E.C. admits these three men died from radiation, because immediately following their overexposure they became sick and died. At least 142 other people overexposed to radiation in the weapons program have died of some form of cancer. But these other men were all latent victims of overexposure, cancer that took a few years to catch up. The agency also refuses to list the many admitted radiation victims employed by prime A.E.C. suppliers. Instead, the burden is on the victim or his heirs to prove that his cancer was radiation-induced. When the victim or his widow comes to court, the A.E.C. has a flock of experts, who just happen to be employed or doing research for the agency, who will testify it is impossible to prove overexposure-caused cancer.

Even the three admitted radiation fatalities are euphemized by the cold-blooded statisticians in the A.E.C.'s Division of Operational Safety. Each fatality is chalked up as a mere "lost-time" accident of 6,000 days. This helps the agency prove that the nuclear industry is safer than industry in general.

The Division of Operational Safety perpetuates this euphemism by regularly reminding employees that nonradiation accidents are their biggest danger. For example, in a December 1, 1970, bulletin to employees, the safety experts headlined a story called "Design Reduces Hazards of Sitting." It told employees that "when office chairs or stools break, injuries to employees are usually minor, but the cost to management—both for preventing similar breaks to similar chairs and for repairing or replacing the broken chairs with new ones—is not only unbelievably high, but totally unnecessary." It concluded that "if we are to protect the sitters from potentially serious back, neck and head injuries, better designs must be provided in chairs and stools. If thousands of dollars are spent recruiting scientific and technical personnel, it seems logical to provide reasonably safe chairs for them. . . . In the meantime, sit carefully."

One reason the agency can claim that nonradiation hazards

are the major source of injury is its refusal to list over 140 uranium miner cancer fatalities in its statistics. The experts explain that since the miners are not directly employed by the commission their deaths do not merit inclusion in agency mortality records. Another reason is that the agency has refused to perform a comprehensive epidemiological study that would show the occupational-cancer rate in the weapons business. As the prime sponsor of nuclear research, the A.E.C. simply refuses to bankroll the work, so it is not done. This makes it impossible to calculate the true effect of the weapons program. However, the need for such a study is certainly pointed to by the number of nuclear pioneers who died prematurely of cancer. Enrico Fermi has already been mentioned. There were also four men who worked at the Berkeley radiation laboratory during World War II who fit into this category. One was William Twitchell, a field engineer who died of a brain tumor on March 3, 1953, at the age of thirty-six. Another was Dr. Joseph Kennedy, a chemistry professor who later worked at Los Alamos and George Washington University before dying of cancer on May 5, 1957, at the age of thirty-nine. There was also Dr. Bertram Low-Beer, a radiologist who came to the United States from England to study with John Lawrence and work for the radiology department of the University of California medical school. He died of leukemia on September 25, 1955, at the age of fifty-five. The fourth victim was Dr. Joseph Hamilton, who worked with fission products from the 60-inch Berkeley cyclotron and served as professor of radiology at the University of California medical school. He died of leukemia on February 18, 1957, at the age of forty-nine. In his obituary the university said it believed he had contracted his fatal disease as a result of his work; although, it added, no episode in which he was overexposed was known to have taken place. The case was listed as an industrial accident.

At least two of the Air Force pilots who flew through radioactive clouds on monitoring assignments during the 1950s are known to have died of leukemia. They are William Wahler and Marvin Speer. Major Richard Patrick, a third member of this aerial monitoring group out of Kirtland Air Force Base, New Mexico, had to have his jaw and part of his larynx removed in 1968 because of cancer. The A.E.C. says that the radiation exposure to the two pilots who died "were well within established limits." It does not say that those limits have since been revised downward. It adds that "no government record has been located on the third pilot. . . . Despite the complex technical task assigned to the commission, the agency has always taken maximum precautions in all nuclear activities to protect both personnel involved and the general public." There are certainly a number of people who would dispute that contention. One of them is a thirty-seven-year-old Cliffwood Beach, New Jersey, dock worker named Edward J. Gleason. On January 8, 1963, Gleason innocently handled an A.E.C. shipment at a Jersey City trucking terminal that contained a liquid solution of hydrochloric acid and gold that had been contaminated by plutonium. The shipment was en route to the A.E.C.'s Brookhaven Laboratory on Long Island where it was to be prepared for disposal.

The story behind the handling of this particular shipment tells a good deal about the A.E.C.'s attitude toward occupational safety. According to a 37-page A.E.C. division of inspection report by Anson M. Bartlett, dated April 11, 1963, this radioactive cargo was hauled through the nation's largest metropolitan area three separate times in violation of A.E.C., Interstate Commerce Commission and Port Authority of New York regulations. The mistakes began on December 30, 1959, when an A.E.C. employee transported the contaminated solution in a glass jug by car from Newark, New Jersey, where it was being held, to the A.E.C.'s New York operations office in Manhattan, via the Holland Tunnel. The method of transportation, packaging and failure to obtain certain permits all violated strict regulations.

Then on March 25, the glass jug containing this dangerous solution was taken to the Nuclear Materials and Equipment Corp. (NUMEC) in Apollo, Pennsylvania, this time in a truck carrying other scrap materials, again via the Holland Tunnel and again in violation of regulations. NUMEC stored the shipment, known as Lot 61, until January 4, 1963, when, at the request of the A.E.C. the jug (known as a carboy) was dispatched to the agency's Brookhaven Laboratory where it would be readied for disposal. The jug, capped with a loosely-fitted rubber stopper and packed in a wooden crate, arrived for transfer to Brookhaven at the Eazor Express Corporation Trucking Terminal in Jersey City on January 8, 1963. It was Gleason, a dock worker for Eazor, who noticed that the box containing Lot 61 was leaking. He was used to handling leaky shipments, so he simply tilted the box onto a handcart and took it to the loading dock. When the box continued to leak, forming a puddle, Gleason turned it over. The dripping stopped and at the suggestion of terminal manager, Richard Grosscost, Gleason covered the puddle with sawdust. Off went the shipment, still leaking, to Brookhaven.

A.E.C. officials finally discovered the leak and became alarmed. The shipment, containing dangerous radioactive material, had not been labeled properly, had not been packaged properly and had not been transported properly. Retracing the route of the shipment, the A.E.C. spent $25,000 decontaminating trucks, truck trailers and terminals. Details of the cleanup made all the newspapers, and ten days after handling the shipment, Gleason read about it in the *Newark News*. He telephoned the A.E.C. and learned that he had indeed handled the contaminated box.

The A.E.C. promptly interviewed Gleason. He said that "at no time did he see a radiation warning label on the box and he had no knowledge that it contained radioactive material. He said he did not see many markings on the box which looked like a used one"—which it was. The A.E.C. report concluded that "Transportation of the plutonium contaminated solution . . . between Newark and New York, between New York and Apollo (Pa.) and between Apollo and Upton, N.Y. violated I.C.C. regulations and Port Authority of New York regulations. . . . I.C.C. regulations were also violated by NUMEC in that a blue radiation warning label . . . showed that the box contained uranium whereas the label should have shown the box contained plutonium." This last point was important because a plutonium shipment of this kind is far more dangerous than a uranium shipment.

Three years after the accident Gleason developed cancer and in 1968 doctors were forced to amputate his left hand, arm and part of his shoulder. Doctors then began giving him cobalt treatments to try to arrest the disease. However this did little good and his condition worsened steadily. Gleason filed suit in the Newark Federal Court of Judge Anthony T. Augelli, asking for 2 million dollars' damages from the A.E.C. and the six companies involved in the mishap. The A.E.C.'s Dr. Arthur Tamplin thinks Gleason has a very good case. He says the chances are "100,000 to one that Gleason's cancer was caused by the contamination. An almost invisible drop of that solution he handled contains enough plutonium to cause frequent cancers in experimental animals." But in December 1970 Judge Augelli dismissed the case on a motion from the defendants. Gleason's lawyers appealed to the 3rd Circuit Court of Appeals in Philadelphia.

Edward Gleason is but one of the many victims of agency negligence. The largest concentration can be found in the uranium mining region of the Colorado Plateau where the states of Colorado, Utah, New Mexico and Arizona share common borders. Miners here have died simply because the government and the mining companies refused to apply well-established clinical data on the radiation hazards of uranium miners. Federal officials estimate 500 to 1,100 of the 6,000 who have been uranium miners will die of lung cancer within the next 20 years because of excessive radiation exposure. By 1970 a total of 142 uranium miners had died from lung cancer. They are the victims of alpha radiation coming from radon-daughters. These daughters are the by-product of decayed uranium ore in the mines. The uranium naturally decays into radium, which gives off radon gas, which in turn gives off the carcinogenic radon-daughters.

Years before uranium mining moved into high gear on the Colorado plateau, the nature of this hazard was documented by European scientists. During the 1930s a study showed that 65 percent of the uranium miners in the Erzebirge mountains of Germany and Czechoslovakia were dying of lung cancer. Another study, between 1935 and 1939, showed half the miners' deaths were from lung cancer and 80 percent of the noncancer deaths were from lung diseases such as tuberculosis, silicosis, emphysema and chronic bronchitis.

These studies prompted the International Commission on Radiation Protection to establish standards for maximum permissible radon exposure in the mines. But the standards were largely ignored in the postwar uranium boom on the Colorado plateau. The A.E.C. hiked the price for uranium oxide from one dollar and 60 cents per pound to an incentive level of 18 dollars per pound, and eager miners went to work.

Soon the U. S. Public Health Service was at work and it had bad news. In 1952 the Public Health Service found that 65 percent of the miners were exposed to concentrations of radon and its daughters comparable to those reported to have existed earlier in European mines. Checks of radon level at 79 mines showed concentrations ranging from two to 59 times the permissible level. A 1955 report by the P.H.S. showed that, of 400 samples taken in 75 mines, radon concentrations ranged between 20 and 230 times the internationally acceptable level.

This data was generally ignored until 1967, when the Industrial Commission of Colorado began to worry about the rising number of claims from widows of uranium miners. After paying out 167,829 dollars to ten widows, the commission asked a New York firm to predict the value of future claims it could expect from miners' widows. The report concluded that the commission would face 8.5 million dollars in claims, a figure that could lead the commission to bankruptcy.

This fact, plus growing reports of miners' deaths, began to attract national press attention. The story finally broke into headlines on April 26, 1967, when atomic-energy consultant Leo Goodman spoke of it in a Washington speech. He detailed the crisis and argued that "over 10,000 underground miners [had been] exposed to one or more 'Holifield' units. I define one 'Holifield' as that amount of underground exposure which is sufficient to give the statistical chance of 60 percent of lung cancer development following the latent period of 7–27 years."

California Congressman Chet Holifield, a charter member of the J.C.A.E., who has traditionally alternated as chairman with Senator John Pastore of Rhode Island, was furious. He scheduled hearings on May 9, 1967, to study "radiation exposure of uranium miners." But before the hearings could open, President Johnson instructed Labor Secretary Willard Wirtz to implement health standards in the mines that would bring the uranium-miner lung-cancer rate down to the national average. Secretary Wirtz promptly issued an order that by January 1, 1969, all radon-gas levels in the mines must be reduced from the allowable maximum of one working level to 0.3 working level (a working level is commonly agreed upon as a measure of exposure to radon-daughters containing a specified concentration of radionuclides).

When the J.C.A.E. hearings began on May 9, 1967, Congressman Holifield was still smarting from newspaper editorials that suggested the J.C.A.E. did not care about miner safety: "Maybe we have not moved fast enough. But maybe we didn't know how to move fast. . . . I want the record to show the uncertainties of knowledge which have existed during the past 15 or 20 years that we have been mining uranium in this country."

Holifield was trying to ignore completely the 1930 European reports that fully explained the carcinogenic effects of radon-daughters on uranium miners. The real culprit, as Secretary Wirtz pointed out in his opening statement to the J.C.A.E., was the dawdling bureaucrats: "The record reflects continuing attention by a variety of state and federal agencies, including the Department of Labor, to both the standards and the inspection problems in connection with uranium mining. It is a record, nevertheless, of literally hundreds of efforts, studies, meetings, conferences, and telephone calls, each of them leading only to another, most of them containing a sufficient reason for not doing anything then, but adding up over a period of years to totally unjustifiable lack of needed consummative action."

Holifield was naturally furious at Wirtz's decision to issue the new working standard for the mines and called on his favored euphemists to back up the J.C.A.E. The prime witness, cited again and again in the J.C.A.E.'s hearing summary, was Dr. Robley Evans, who identified himself as a professor of physics at M.I.T. as well as a consultant to the Office of Scientific Research and Development, the Army, the Air Force, the Navy, the U. S. Public Health Service, the State Department, the Secretary of Defense, the Research and Development Board of the National Military Establishment, the Federal Radiation Council, and the Division of Biology and Medicine of the Atomic Energy Commission. But nowhere in the biography was any mention that Dr. Evans was a consultant with Kerr-McGee Corporation, one of America's largest uranium producers.

Dr. Evans told J. V. Reistrup of the *New Republic* that he had never billed any organization for his work on the uranium miners. But when the hearing was over, the A.E.C. boosted its grant for Dr. Evans' project at M.I.T. to 174,919 dollars.

Secretary Wirtz also was chided by the Federal Radiation Council, which recommended in a September 1967 report that the miners be allowed continued exposure to one working level. A.E.C. scientists John Gofman and Arthur Tamplin replied that this would roughly double the lung-cancer rate among men who worked in the mines for eight years. But the F.R.C. argued the laxity was justified by mitigating circumstances. The council pointed out that uranium is "an important economic asset to the states in which it is mined and that mining provides important employment opportunities."

This argument did not dissuade Secretary Wirtz, who insisted on implementing the 0.3 working-level standard through installation of improved ventilation equipment that would reduce the amount of the radioactive gas in mines. Congressman Holifield, of course, was again furious and complained about the milksop "Secretaries of the Department of Health, Education and Welfare and some others [Wirtz]. . . . These people are laymen. They are not technically qualified, and this is one of the things that has bothered this committee because we say . . . the [new] standards for the operation of the [uranium] mines . . . was set [by Wirtz] . . . on an emotional basis rather than on a scientific basis." Wirtz, of course, was a mere transient cabinet official, whose will was thwarted after he left office. The Federal Radiation Council, which was absorbed by the Environmental Protection Agency, managed to stall final implementation of the tighter standard into 1971. Despite the growing number of miner corpses on the Colorado plateau, the experts said they could not reach a decision by the December 31, 1971, deadline. So President Nixon gave them and the uranium-mining industry a six-month extension, to July 1, 1971.

But even when effective standards are finally imposed on the uranium mines, the men who work in them will not be fully protected. The miners, their families and neighbors who live in or near these uranium mill towns are plagued by another health hazard, thanks to official negligence. Over the years the mills have sold and given away their radioactive waste for use as landfill beneath schools, homes, stores and other structures numbering in the thousands. These radioactive wastes, known as "tailings," emit the very same radon gas that caused the high lung-cancer rate among the miners. Because the radon emitted by the tailings seeps up through the building foundations, occupants are now breathing "indoor radon." This has prompted federal and state officials to comb through hundreds of homes in the uranium mill towns of western Colorado to pinpoint high indoor radon levels. Like the prospectors who originally discovered uranium ore on the Colorado plateau, the health experts come armed with scintillation counters to pinpoint the radioactive tailings beneath the structures. It is a tough job, because no one kept any records on which structures were built over tailings. Thus in Grand Junction, Colorado, a town of 18,000, teams are checking 6,500 buildings. By the fall of 1970 nearly one out of five buildings tested showed high levels.

Although evacuations in Grand Junction will await further study, some victims of indoor radon have already been moved. In January 1970, the Union Carbide Corporation evacuated two families from company-owned homes in the mining town of Uravan after a check showed that radon levels inside their homes were 160 to 710 times the recommended maximum, which is higher than maximum exposure levels permitted in uranium mines. It seems that both homes were situated directly atop actual tailings piles left by former mills at the site.

The tailings pile at Uravan is one of 35 located across nine Western states from Texas to Oregon. The Environmental Protection Agency estimates these piles have about 90,589,000 tons of tailings, primarily on the Colorado plateau. Although tailings are no longer being hauled away for landfill, children in Uravan continue to play on a neighborhood pile. Another pile, in Salt Lake City, is easily accessible to the public. In Arizona and Utah abandoned mill tailings blight a Navajo Indian reservation. Health officials say high radiation levels make the tailings areas too dangerous for public use.

Incredibly the official move to protect people from indoor radon did not get moving until nearly ten years after the government got involved in checking the spread of tailings. In fact, in the late 1950s when the U. S. Public Health Service began clamping down on disposal of mill tailings into streams, the mill owners were still actively selling and giving away these very same tailings as landfill.

Any high-school student reading the data on tailings contamination of the streams could have easily seen the hazard of giving the tailings away for landfill. In 1958–59, for example, the Animas River, which forms the principal water supply for the 30,000 people of Aztec and Farmington, New Mexico, had dissolved radium contents averaging five to eight times the background level. River-bottom fauna studies in the Animas in the summer of 1958 showed virtual elimination of life immediately below Durango and severe damage as far downstream as 50 miles. Later studies of the San Miguel and Dolores Rivers below the Uravan mill showed that dissolved radium ranged 50 to 300 times background. Radium in sediments ranged from 20 to 50 times background and there was a substantial reduction in the fish population on the San Miguel below the Uravan mill. Six of the species formerly present were not found in this study by Utah State University.

More important, the contaminated radium sediments had been transported downstream into the large reservoirs on the Colorado River, which supplies water for California, New Mexico, Nevada, Utah, Wyoming, Colorado and Arizona. The Public Health Service study of sediments in the Lake Mead reservoir showed radium concentrations three times the background level of the basin streams.

These grim data led the Public Health Service to force mills to cease dumping radioactive effluent into the streams. As a result, radium contamination of the Colorado River basin was reduced by the end of the 1960s. But the stabilization is not foolproof. Simply spraying the tailings with oil or covering them with dirt is not sure protection against wind and rain. Erosion continues to carry tailings into watersheds for many miles.

What makes all these tailings especially troublesome is the long-lived nature of the radium content, which has a radioactive half-life of 1,600 years. To safeguard present and future generations, the country needs to stabilize all piles, pinpoint where tailings have been used and get people out of buildings where contamination levels are dangerous.

State-health officials, traditionally understaffed and underfinanced, are just beginning to catch up with the problem. For example, in Utah, public-health officials are in the process of implementing a new regulation that would force four companies to stabilize tailings piles. But Utah's radiation health chief, Dennis Dalley, says there are no immediate plans to search for tailings used as construction fill: "At this time we know of no specific instances where tailings have been used as fill."

However, a number of buildings rest atop mill tailings within five miles of the Utah Division of Health offices. The radioactive debris came from the tailings pile of the Vitro Corporation of America mill located in an industrial area just south of Salt Lake City. During the 1950s, thousands of tons of tailings were released for construction fill. Local contractors used the radioactive tailings for fill beneath a fire station, warehouse, meat-packing plant, gas station, sewage plant and other buildings. These structures include the Salt Lake County fire station at 3690 South Main, Shuttercraft Wood Products, A and R Meats, and the Suburban Sanitary District sewage plant.

Jim Moore, who managed the Vitro Mill in Salt Lake City until it closed in 1968, can remember half a dozen separate occasions when the tailings were sold to contractors for a nominal price. Moore, who is now with the Anaconda Company in Salt Lake City, says: "We let people take these tailings with the complete written authorization of the Atomic Energy Commission." Harold Breitling, a local excavator based near the defunct mill, remembers hauling fill from the Vitro pile in the 1950s. "The tailings were a lot cheaper than fill we would have had to buy elsewhere." Eldon K. Fuller, another Salt Lake City excavator, says: "The fill was used by a lot of people around here. I refused to buy any of the mill tailings because I thought they might pose some sort of radiation hazard. One time I was outbid on a job by a competitor who saved money by using the inexpensive mill tailings for fill." Theo Wood, who used to live behind the Vitro mill in the 1950s, clearly remembers customers coming by to pick up the tailings. Wood, who now lives in Mesa, Arizona, says: "I used to stand and watch the dump trucks drive in and haul tons of tailings away for use as fill."

At the Salt Lake County fire station on South Main Street battallion chief Shirl Maxfield says: "When they began building our station in 1957 mill tailings were used as fill to a depth of three feet." The 33 firemen employed by the department show no concern about the potential hazard posed by the tailings underfoot. The department rotation system means that ten men live in the fire station at any one time.

Although contractors are no longer allowed to remove tailings from the Vitro pile, the radioactive waste continues to be a part of Salt Lake City. While some of the nonradioactive debris has been stabilized, the radium-bearing mill tailings continue to be eroded by high winds. Since Vitro left the town in 1968, little attention has been paid to the pile. A small barbed-wire fence falls short of the northwest boundary of the tailings heap. One can walk out onto the tailings pile unimpeded. The lone detective-agency guard assigned to the plant can't possibly keep track of the vast pile all at once.

The man in charge of the abandoned Salt Lake mill is Vitro's Richard Miller. Formerly assistant manager in Salt Lake City, he is now with Vitro's industrial-engineering division in Portland. Miller seemed flabbergasted when he was told that the tailings were used beneath Salt Lake City buildings: "That's the first time I've ever heard about it. As far as I knew the only place tailings were used was at the sewage plant adjacent to the mill. Of course, I was away from Salt Lake [City] for a number of years—maybe this happened when I wasn't around." Miller is hopeful that some records may exist on disposition of the tailings: "We've probably got some kind of a report on where the tailings went. It might be in our vault inside the plant in Salt Lake [City], I'm not really certain." And the existing tailings pile? "Well, the state highway department is widening a road on the south boundary of the plant. They will take 50,000 yards of excavation and dump it on top of the pile. That should stabilize it."

Of course, Utah is only one of the Western states troubled by tailings. Colorado, which has led the way on the tailings cleanup, is just starting to catch up with the vast problem. Federal funds and manpower have helped the state push tailings studies in seven mill towns. In Grand Junction the work is being expedited by deploying state health experts pulled off other assignments. But even with extra manpower the work goes very slowly. Nearly all 3,000 Grand Junction buildings built between 1950 and 1966 were erected on tailings furnished by the local American Metal Climax mill. So the health inspectors are checking every single building for dangerous radiation levels. By the fall of 1970 some 95 buildings registered high readings. These buildings are being further evaluated as the experts decide whether to evacuate, modify or leave them alone.

Health experts who have been studying the prevalent cancer among uranium miners have moved into Grand Junction for a look at residents of homes built on mill tailings. The Environmental Protection Agency is sending some residents of Colorado homes to Los Alamos for radiation-exposure tests. And Dr. Geno Saccomanno, a Grand Junction pathologist specializing in radiation health, is working on a chromosomal study on occupants of these buildings. Dr. Saccomanno says he has "done these studies on miners who were overexposed to radiation. I'd like to find out what has happened to these residents."

Occupants of buildings that showed high radon levels on preliminary tests seem calm. For example, the Seventh Day Adventist Intermountain Junior Academy merely evacuated its two-room addition that sits on mill tailings. There was no public announcement. And some Grand Junction residents seem downright defensive about the tailings. Harry Lidikay, whose Texaco station showed a high radon level, says one of his best customers heads the A.E.C. office in Grand Junction: "You know, the last time I saw him he was worried about the turn signal on his car. He didn't say anything about tailings. I figure if he's not worried about tailings, then I'm not worried."

It seems that traditionally no one in the A.E.C. has worried very much about tailings. Donald Nussbaumer, chief of the A.E.C.'s Source and Special Nuclear Materials Branch, explains why: "By law we have never had regulatory authority over mill tailings. Only materials that are .05 percent uranium and thorium by weight are subject to A.E.C. authority. Mill tailings are generally composed of .02 percent uranium and thorium so we aren't responsible for them." The A.E.C.'s sole defense is an informal effort made to keep uranium mills and state health departments in affected regions aware of potential tailings hazards. On March 7, 1961, Harold Price, then director of the Division of Licensing and Regulation, wrote a letter to the relevant mills and states pointing out that "the transfer of sand mill tailings for uses such as road building would not . . . be within the commission's regulatory control. And such uses would not be an integral part of the milling operation. We are calling this fact to your attention because . . . the radium content of these tailings might be such as to warrant control by appropriate state authorities of particular uses of tailings having a significant radium content."

Today the A.E.C.'s Mr. Nussbaumer says: "In retrospect it now appears someone should have kept central records on the use of the tailings. It would have been better if these wastes were watched more closely." One of the reasons Mr. Nussbaumer feels this way is that new research makes the tailings problem look worse and worse. Robert Snelling of the Environmental Protection Agency in Las Vegas has found that a number of tailings piles on Indian reservations are causing problems. For example, late in 1969 Snelling issued a study of the uranium-tailings pile next to a mill operated by the A-Z Minerals Corporation in Mexican Hat, Utah. The now defunct mill is located on a Navajo reservation and the Indians wanted to know if they could resume public use of the area. In his study, Snelling found external gamma radiation on the tailings area with nine times the recommended maximum. As a result he concluded that "the external radiation levels on the tailings area exceed recommended exposure limits for individuals in the general population. Therefore, the area should not be released for public use in its present state."

Snelling reached the same conclusion after studying an El Paso Natural Gas Company tailings pile near Tuba City, Arizona, in 1967. Here, too, the mill was on Navajo property and the Indians wanted to resume use of the abandoned site. But Snelling found extensive radiation that precluded public use. Gamma radiation on the mill tailings area was 12 times the recommended maximum. Wind carriage of the tailings elevated gamma radiation to the maximum level within 1,000 feet of the property fence. Airborne particulate sampling found three times the maximum permissible radium level and ten times the maximum thorium level 200 feet east of the mill property. To maximize public safety, Snelling has recommended that these piles and another tailings heap on a Navajo reservation at Monument Valley, Arizona (where radiation levels did not exceed recommended exposure limits) be stabilized against wind erosion.

Tailings stabilization is a difficult business. In 1963 the A.E.C. moved to stabilize a tailings pile next to its former mill in Monticello, Utah. The work was done at great expense, but minor washouts have eroded the cover and necessitated maintenance work. Utah's radiation health chief, Dennis Dalley, reports that gophers have chewed off some of the cover and kicked tailings back on top of the Monticello pile. Of course, there are other ways of disposing uranium-mill wastes. Since 1960 the Anaconda Company uranium mill at Bluewater, New Mexico, has been pumping about 150 gallons of radioactive waste per minute into a 1,830-foot well for the past ten years. Plant manager Albert Fitch says: "Things have gone very smoothly from the beginning. We have a continuing testing program at nearby potable-water wells and there is no sign of any contamination or leakage."

However, some experts, such as geologist David Evans, a director of the Colorado School of Mines Mineral Resources Institute, have reservations about this well system: "The fact that the poisons haven't shown up anywhere in ten years doesn't mean they are home free. What happens in 30 years if these radioactive wastes start coming up out of the ground or turn up in someone's drinking water? Fourteen percent of the 114 industrial disposal wells in this country have failed for one reason or another. The blowout in the Santa Barbara channel suggests the potential of a defective well. And we shouldn't forget Buffalo, New York, where cyanide escaped from a disposal well into drinking water, or Erie, Pennsylvania, where another well failure poured 150,000 gallons of sulfite liquor into Lake Erie every day for three weeks. Millions of gallons of radioactive waste have now been pumped beneath New Mexico. What do we do if, despite all safety precautions, they get out?"

There is probably only one cheerful thought attached to the subject of uranium-mill tailings. It is not too late. There is still time to stabilize the piles, find where the tailings have been used and evacuate residents of contaminated houses. Some officials think evacuation may not be necessary in certain situations. For example, Robert Snelling of the Environmental Protection Agency says: "Perhaps fans can be installed in crawl spaces beneath some of the contaminated homes. They would provide extra ventilation and reduce the amount of radon seeping up into the house." And in Grand Junction, Dr. Geno Saccomanno suggests that "the contaminated houses be jacked up for a day. Then all the tailings can be scraped out from underneath and replaced by nonradioactive dirt."

PROMOTION

The Pentagon and the A.E.C. have several hundred men posted throughout the world who can rush to the scene of a nuclear-weapons accident at a moment's notice. They know how to evacuate the neighborhood, cordon off the area, monitor for contamination and pick up the pieces. One of the senior A.E.C. scientists who helps cleanup is Dr. Wright Langham. Dr. Langham is a leading expert on the radiation effects of nuclear weapons and has been with the Los Alamos Laboratory since World War II. When nuclear weapons were accidentially dropped on Palomares, Spain, in January 1966, he was rushed in to monitor plutonium contamination. The following year Dr. Langham was awarded the Pentagon's Distinguished Service Medal for his work. And in January 1968 he was back on the accident scene when another armed nuclear bomber crashed, at Thule, Greenland.

Looking back on his distinguished career in a December 1968 paper written for the Department of Health, Education and Welfare, Dr. Langham cited "two very good personal reasons . . . why plutonium is my favorite element. Upon completing my schooling in the spring of 1943, I was given the choice of joining the Manhattan project . . . to work on plutonium or accepting a

1-A draft card." He selected the Manhattan project, and "since that time the reputation of plutonium as a toxic material perhaps has contributed more than any other thing to my being supported in the modest though comfortable manner to which I have grown accustomed."

This is the bright side of the bomb; every fallout cloud does have a silver lining. No one, least of all Dr. Langham, argues that the bomb is foolproof. But if you have got to have a nuclear defense, let's take some pride in it and think positively. That is certainly the attitude of the men in the Defense Department and the A.E.C. who spend their time protecting the bomb's image. Through the Sandia museum, movies, books, press releases, speeches and road shows, they try to promote the image of safe, reliable bombs. It is a tricky job that entails a careful balance between showmanship and censorship. The general maxim is to cover up the past and promote the future. Thus, on the one hand, reporters and congressmen are taken on a tour of a Kansas salt mine proposed as an eminently safe site for the burial of nuclear garbage, but when the National Academy of Sciences complains that current A.E.C. waste-disposal tanks are leaking, the agency conveniently suppresses the charges.

The A.E.C. does not like to admit that some scientists believe nuclear-weapons testing can be dangerous. That is why it retains right of approval over agency-related public-health studies conducted by the Environmental Protection Agency and the National Academy of Science. An A.E.C. advisory committee that submits a report unfavorable to the agency may be dissolved and replaced with a friendlier committee representing a "broader spectrum of scientific disciplines." When A.E.C. scientists do criticize the weapons program, their superiors try to "help" them rewrite their reports in a more palatable form. If this does not work, the scientists may find their reports being censored, their staff budgets eviscerated or their careers jeopardized by being blacklisted.

Periodically A.E.C. scientists are assigned to do hatchet jobs on reports unfavorable to the image of the weapons program. But if the critiques are not completely critical, the brass may try to censor them, too. When political pressure forces reexamination of the status quo, the work is coded under the vaguest title possible. Thus a study on carcinogenic effects of strontium 90 in fallout is labeled "Project Sunshine."

Since the A.E.C. directly or indirectly finances the major research, publishing and film activities in atomic energy, it can easily obviate history unfavorable to the bomb's image. Schools and church groups that want a film on the bombing of Hiroshima and Nagaski can get one from the A.E.C. called *A Tale of Two Cities.* The vast agency film library also has travelogues such as *Return to Bikini,* in which scientists visit past victims of agency test fallout. The official, subsidized *History of the U.S. AEC 1939–46* boasts that the co-authors are the only ones who have ever enjoyed access to all the (agency) records, including classified material. Yet the book does not cover such vital bits of history as the deaths of Los Alamos scientists Harry Daghlian and Louis Slotin following criticality accidents.

As the nation's primary purveyor of atomic-energy information, the agency publishes a long bibliography of "Books on Atomic Energy." Naturally any volume that critically evaluates some phase of the nuclear business is omitted. Thus a book such as *Lawrence and Oppenheimer* can win rave reviews from the major publications but not merit a mention in the A.E.C. bibliography. When a writer asks why the book is omitted, an A.E.C. public-relations man promptly dredges up a couple of reviews from obscure publications which flail the book for putting down the nuclear establishment. A scholar such as Ralph Lapp, who has turned out numerous fine books on all phases of the weapons business gets a mention for only one of his 12 titles and that is a book aimed at high-school students. Lapp's brilliant report *The Voyage of The Lucky Dragon,* his invaluable primer *Radiation* (with Jack Schubert) and his study *The Weapons Culture* are all conveniently omitted. Naturally all the works of authors such as Glenn T. Seaborg are listed. If you are too busy to go to the library, the A.E.C. will be delighted to send his collected speeches free of charge.

Creating the right image for the bomb involves a careful promotional campaign that began with the Manhattan Project. Over the six years that the bomb was being developed, the scientific community enjoyed the benefits of complete censorship. They were able to do their job without any interference by public opinion. The entire decision to build, test and use the bomb was made by the politicians and the scientists. No one was allowed to breathe words that might hint at development of the bomb. Army censors ordered media to avoid words such as "atomic energy" or "Los Alamos." Articles dealing with atomic energy in any way were watched nervously. In 1943 squeamish Army security leaders asked the *Saturday Evening Post* immediately to report any reprint requests received for a 1940 issue that contained an article by *The New York Times* reporter William L. Laurence on atomic energy. They feared enemy agents might use it for intelligence purposes. The *Post* was asked to delay mailing copies of this back number until it received instructions from the Manhattan Project officials. This calmed the generals, who were apparently oblivious to the fact that enemy agents could get back issues of the *Post* by simply going to the library.

When it came time to announce the bomb, the Manhattan Project hired Laurence, a *New York Times* science writer, secretly to cover the final stages of bomb development, testing and combat use. Laurence was a reporter who wrote dramatic publicity pieces for the Army and brilliant pieces for the *Times* at the same time. For the next decade the weapons program would enjoy a relatively warm relationship with the press, partially because of the cold war, partially because of security and partially because of the public fascination with this strange and powerful weapon.

But in the late 1950s fallout fears, doomsday books such as *On the Beach* and the cold-war thaw began to convince the public that nuclear weapons could be an internal threat. The A.E.C. decided to boost the bomb's image by demonstrating its manifold peacetime applications. But the nuclear sword did not make a very good plowshare. The first civilian nuclear test was "Project Gnome" in Carlsbad, New Mexico, in December 1961. Shortly before detonation time the A.E.C. passed out a pamphlet stating that the probability of a venting was nil. But when the bomb was triggered, a thick white vapor puffed through an elevator shaft and slowly spread like ground fog. The impossible venting had happened. An A.E.C. officer told drivers to turn their cars around to facilitate a speedy retreat from the area. At a roadblock in Carlsbad seven cars were found contaminated and later were decontaminated. When it was over, an A.E.C. official told writer Daniel Lang that the explosion originally planned to yield ten kilotons but was cut down to five kilotons: "Whoever made that decision, I'd like to shake his hand."

Reporters also began catching slips in agency reports. In the Nevada test site's NVO-40 report a federal geologist said underground formations in one region of the shot "dictated" a maximum shot depth less than some that had already been used. The A.E.C. later explained the statement was merely an unaccountable editing error and issued a revised report with this key criticism eliminated.

Sometimes the truth inadvertently slips out to the embarrassment of the entire A.E.C. information staff. For example, the United States, like Russia, does not announce all its nuclear tests. Presumably this is for security, although experts say that both Russia and the United States hide roughly the same percentage of tests, so the net effect of secrecy is zero. Nonetheless, officials persist in hiding the number of tests and this has caused a credibility gap of sorts. On August 20, 1963, President Kennedy announced a number of American nuclear tests 23 higher than the public record. The official number of tests was simply raised 23 without comment.

The A.E.C. prefers not to have the public think of all these tests as vast mushroom clouds, but as sober experiments designed to advance science and the goals of man. This, of course, often involves rewriting history, particularly in the audiovisual program. A good example is the film *Return to Bikini,* which depicts the remarkable recovery of the Marshall Islands from our nuclear bombings in the 1940s and 1950s. This film, released in 1965, shows University of Washington scientists finding the islands in fine shape: "External radiation on the islands has dropped to levels safe for people, plants are growing again, coconut trees are coming back," the rainwater is safe for drinking, the fish are great. When the script reaches Rongelap, facts of the three-year evacuation following the Bravo accident (see Chapter 3) are glossed over. As this section opens, the scientists are arriving at Rongelap for a visit. (Portions of the original script that were censored in the final version are in parentheses.):

VIDEO:	AUDIO:
Scientists jump from copra boat to beach	The laboratory has studied radioactivity
Scientists greet natives	at Rongelap (since the accident) and
C/u [close up] native's face	the scientists are well-known to the people.
Gum given to children	(The radiation burns are healed, the people are happy to be home.) The children (most of them born since the fallout accident) have a great time
Kids wade in water	in their natural playground. . . . And they know just how
Kids point at boats made of gum wrappers	to make sailboats from chewing gum wrappers. . . .

The scientists go on to study the island's ecology before they load their specimens of pandanus, breadfruit and coconuts aboard the ship. The expedition is leaving Rongelap:

VIDEO:	AUDIO:
Old woman making mat	But memories of the atoll and its resourceful people will remain long after the scientists are
C/u woman's face	back in their university
C/u hands making mat	laboratories. The people (their simple lives changed by an unexpected fallout cloud) are back
Woman washing clothes	to their old self-sufficient ways.
C/u woman's face	Their atoll, once considered hazardously
Woman making mat, two kids watching	radioactive, again provides a livelihood. . . .

C/u same	Nature has erased the radiation hazard at Rongelap; life is back to normal routine. The Rongelap people—clean, sociable, energetic—
C/u hands washing	are wonderfully adapted to atoll life the same as that formerly led by
Woman hands up clothes	their neighbors on Bikini and Eniwetok; . . . the relaxed, rhythmic existence of
Woman playing ukelele	the tropics. Mothers' songs, the shouts and laughter of playing children could be
L/s [long shot] skipping rope	heard even now on all the test islands if radioactivity were the only problem. But these people depend on
M/s [medium shot] girls skip rope	natural food chains extending to the
C/u kids' hands, game	tiniest creatures of the land and
L/s same	sea.
C/u girls' faces at game	At one time, we expected little
Ship off Rongelap	recovery growth on the atolls.
Aerial [view] of atoll	Now, as the expedition leaves, we know that Rongelap is back to normal and remaining damage on Bikini and Eniwetok is rapidly healing—impressive evidence of nature's ability to bounce back—dramatic illustration of nature's toughness and resiliency in the face of forces undreamed of by our forefathers.

Our forefathers probably also never dreamed foolish white men would contaminate their island and then send back film crews to document the resilience of nature. The film manages to avoid completely the key facts of the Rongelap disaster. There is no footage of the 13 natives who had developed thyroid abnormalities by the time the movie was shot in 1965. Nor is there any footage of eight Rongelap natives having all or part of their poisoned thyroids taken out at various American hospitals. But even if these facts had been shown in 1965, *Return to Bikini* would still need to be updated. By the fall of 1970 thyroid abnormalities had increased to 21 and thyroidectomies stood at 18. All but two of the 19 children under ten when the accident happened developed abnormal thyroids. Bikini is nothing for the A.E.C. to be proud of, let alone boast about.

Boosting the bomb's image involves more than just movies and press releases, books, museums and tours for the press. It also means making sure all reports relating to the weapons program support the A.E.C. Robert E. Miller, the manager of the A.E.C.'s Nevada Operations Office, assures the public their safety is never compromised: "My daughter and my grandchildren live in this city [Las Vegas]. When my government makes a decision that national security is involved in this testing, I feel bound to support that commitment to execute the program with the minimum acceptable risk to people and property. But I also feel that I have a responsibility to assure those children's safety. Both those considerations figure in my life every day and I can assure you that so far I've had no trouble reconciling them. . . . There has been no instance in which human injury as a result of radiation from Nevada testing has been established."

Mr. Miller can utter this certitude because the A.E.C. will not sponsor the necessary long-range medical studies to find out what the test program has done to its neighbors in the West. This negligence contradicts a fifteen-year-old recommendation from the Public Health Service. In a 1953 "Official Use Only" report the P.H.S. noted that weapons tests during that year exposed parts of Nevada and Utah to contamination far over the standards of the National Committee on Radiation Protection. In a section the authors called "probably the most significant summary in the report," the P.H.S. said: "In future tests, within such areas, blood changes in man might be demonstrable if systematic observations are made. It is possible also that the immunities of the population might be sufficiently reduced that measurable increased incidences of selected communicable diseases would be discerned by epidemiological investigations. The long-term implications of yearly exposure of a cross-section of the population to levels in excess of those considered to be maximum permissible for occupational workers certainly justify continued observation and maintenance of radiation health records, even though specific consequences cannot be foreseen at this moment."

First, the recommendation was ignored, and then, when the report was declassified, it was deleted. But even if the study was conducted, it is doubtful that the final results would displease the A.E.C. For the agency finances Environmental Protection Agency (formerly Public Health Service) studies on its operation. Dr. Melvin Carter, head of the Southwestern Radiological Laboratory in Las Vegas, which is responsible for offsite monitoring of the weapons tests and the radiological health of the Western states, was asked what happens when the interests of its benefactor and the public collide. He replied, "We're here to represent the public and our clientele are the members of the public."

One of Dr. Carter's jobs is to serve on the group which advises the A.E.C. test manager on the conduct of each test. He says he has never made a recommendation about public safety that has been ignored. But what would happen if Dr. Carter and the A.E.C. disagreed over the content of a report? Dr. Carter does not know, but Henry Vermillion, the veteran public-information officer for the A.E.C.'s Nevada office, says he thinks he does. In an interview with writer Paul Jacobs, Vermillion said that Environmental Protection Agency reports are sent to the A.E.C. "for review which normally is pretty pro forma." But if the A.E.C. personnel disagreed with the report, "there would be a discussion and I assume that in the final analysis, if the man here felt strongly enough, probably it wouldn't get into the report. The key point is who controls, that's always the key point, and I think that under our memorandum of agreement with the Public Health Service (now Environmental Protection Agency) the information is controlled by the A.E.C., because it does support this part of the Public Health Service."

One of the crucial weapons tests reported in the 1953 P.H.S. report became the center of a 1963 dispute between Dr. Harold Knapp and the A.E.C. The test was 32-kiloton shot Harry, which occurred on May 19, 1953. This test (which is covered in chapter 3) deposited heavy fallout in St. George, Utah, a town of 5,000 people about 120 miles east of the test site. The A.E.C. staff was interested in checking for milk contaminated by fission products in the St. George area. But monitors chose not to do it, because they lacked necessary expertise and did not want to scare the public.

In 1960 Dr. Knapp, who was then on the staff of the A.E.C.'s Fallout Studies Branch of the Division of Biology and Medicine, was asked by the A.E.C. to write a report on "The Contribution of Hot Spots and Short-Lived Activities to Radiation Exposure in the U.S. from Nuclear Test Fallout." The study was ordered to help the commission resolve a controversy between its general advisory committee and Ralph Lapp over radiation doses in these hot spots.

Lapp's sharp criticism spurred the commission to speed up Knapp's completion of the report. After sending it to the committee, Knapp made a final review prior to A.E.C. publication and made "a rather startling discovery." The A.E.C. had overlooked the effects of radioactive iodine 131, especially on children's thyroids, concentrating instead on strontium 90 and cesium 137. This oversight happened because the commission had not collected data on the iodine 131 content of milk around the test site from 1951 to 1953.

Knapp set out to discover how much iodine 131 had gone into the St. George milk following the May 19, 1953, test. His superiors, in a hurry to publish the report, tried to discourage him. But Knapp insisted on writing a revised version. His research took him on a personal visit to the region around the Nevada test site, where he was shocked to discover the paucity of off-site monitoring conducted during the 1953 tests. In his revised report Knapp concluded that (1) the A.E.C. had completely failed to monitor for iodine 131, and (2) the dosage of this radionuclide had been underestimated by over 1,000 percent in certain sections of the United States.

When Knapp submitted his report in 1963, the A.E.C. leadership was furious, not with its past inadequacies on iodine 131 research, but with Knapp for breaking the party line. Although some of Knapp's colleagues backed him, the agency brass found the report to be of "questionable technical validity." The real uncertainty, though, was not Knapp's data but the agency's image.

After reading the Knapp report, one A.E.C. staff member told his boss: "The Commission has been telling the world for years that it has been conducting its operations safely. Now it appears this may not be so." The boss wondered out loud: "If a member of the staff says this about the paper, what reaction can we expect from the press and public?" Another A.E.C. leader commented, "We have spent years of hard, patient effort to establish good and calm relations with the public around the Nevada test site. Such actions as the author's have been harmful."

Knapp insisted the report be published, so his superiors looked to other scientists to discredit it. They naturally chose scientists employed by the agency or dependent on it for research support. One of the men brought in to review Knapp's report was John Gofman, who had survived his contamination accident with Glenn Seaborg in 1941 and gone on to pick up a Ph.D., M.D., and professorship of medical physics at the University of California at Berkeley. The A.E.C. had just appointed him associate director of the Livermore Radiation Laboratory and head of a new biomedical program that would study effects of nuclear testing on mankind. Gofman feared establishment of the new laboratory was merely an A.E.C. publicity stunt to help public criticism of the test program's nuclear pollution. But he took the job on the promise of A.E.C. Chairman Seaborg that "all we want is for you to tell the truth about biological and medical hazards. You need have no fear that there would ever be any interference with release of the truth."

The A.E.C. announced the opening of Gofman's lab on May 31, 1963, and a few months later he was called back to Washington for an "important conference" at the Division of Biology and Medicine. The conference was supposedly on the subject of radioactive iodine, but Gofman quickly saw that its purpose was "to figure out a way to squelch Knapp's report." A.E.C. leaders said publishing Knapp's report would discredit all A.E.C. studies on the subject during the past ten years. The committee members met with Knapp and finally recommended releasing the report. But the A.E.C.'s published version omitted Knapp's estimate that the 1953 weapons test had given a dose of 120 to 440 rads to the thyroids of infants in St. George, a very heavy overexposure. Knapp subsequently quit the commission and published his complete report in *Nature* magazine. Dr. Gordon Dunning, director of the A.E.C.'s Division of Operational Safety, was very depressed. He and the agency had given Knapp so much help on his radioiodine study. There were guided tours of the Nevada test site, lessons in monitoring procedures, plus endless consultations aimed at making the report jibe with the A.E.C.'s and the Public Health Service's past platitudes: "We were trying to help him and his report," said Dunning afterward. "If he'd stuck with us a little longer, we might have gotten it into a form that we'd all agree to."

Patience is required of anyone trying to write a report that contradicts the A.E.C.'s public image. Take nuclear waste disposal, one of the A.E.C.'s most critical problems. The agency has set aside vast nuclear graveyards at Hanford, Washington; Arco, Idaho; Aiken, South Carolina; and Oak Ridge, Tennessee. Hundreds of square miles have been permanently condemned as repositories for long-lived radioactive waste. The agency desperately needs more space for disposing of the growing amount of nuclear garbage. The Rocky Flats fire alone generated over 330,000 cubic yards of radioactive garbage, which was shipped to Idaho via train. There is also a pressing need for better disposal techniques since some of the pioneer burial grounds have been spilling waste. Between 1944 and 1970, 11 of the 149 nuclear-waste storage tanks at Hanford have sprung leaks. About 50,000 gallons of radioactive waste poured from one tank.

To help plan better waste-disposal practices, the agency has relied on the National Academy of Sciences' National Research Council, Earth Sciences Division, to serve in an advisory capacity on radioactive-waste management. In May of 1966 the council's Committee on Geological Aspects of Radioactive Waste Disposal sent a report to the A.E.C. which concluded (1) that all four of the agency's major waste-disposal sites were "in poor geological locations" and (2) that none of the agency's waste-disposal practices satisfied the committee's safety criteria. The A.E.C., which funded the report, also suppressed it. Three successive chairmen of the G.A.R.W.D. tried to get the report released without success.

In 1968 the A.E.C. asked the National Academy of Sciences to dissolve the G.A.R.W.D. committee and replace it with a new group representing a "broader spectrum of scientific disciplines" called the Committee on Radioactive Waste Management. This was handy in 1970, when the A.E.C. was finally forced into issuing the 1966 G.A.R.W.D. report. In releasing the report, the A.E.C. attached an interim report from the new, more obedient committee, which reported on a series of visits to radioactive-waste dumps: "The Committee noted the extensiveness and care in waste management at each site visited. The Committee is gratified by the quality and scope of the R & D program sponsored by the A.E.C. in radioactive-waste management." The A.E.C. also attached a staff paper saying that implementation of the safety recommendations in the critical 1966 report would have cost billions, far more than the agency could afford.

Trading in an unfavorable advisory committee for a favorable one is a good way to save face. But when a critic wins national publicity, the agency likes to call in one of its top scientists for a hatchet job. This happened in the spring of 1969, when University of Pittsburgh scientist Ernest J. Sternglass raised the most serious criticism of the weapons program since the fallout crisis in the 1950s. In a report widely publicized by the mass media and later published in *Esquire* magazine under the title "The Death of All Children," Dr. Sternglass charged that nuclear-test fallout had caused 400,000 excess prenatal and infant mortalities. The A.E.C. immediately turned to its Livermore Biomedical Division and asked Dr. Arthur Tamplin to do a critique of the Sternglass report. Tamplin was certainly a good choice. The biophysicist had pioneered the standard technique for measuring nuclear-test fallout patterns that is used by scientists throughout the world. Dr. Tamplin agreed, and presented his paper before a Livermore symposium in April 1969. He had good news for the A.E.C. Tamplin declared that Sternglass had drastically overestimated the effects of the fallout. He calculated that fallout had caused only 4,000 excess infant and prenatal fatalities, just one percent of Sternglass' figure.

After the symposium Tamplin proceeded to write his report as an A.E.C. technical paper and submit it to his boss, John Totter, head of the A.E.C.'s Division of Biology and Medicine. Surprisingly Totter was not pleased with the slashing critique of Sternglass. He tried to persuade Tamplin to delete a section from the paper. In a phone call on August 13, Totter and Spofford English, an assistant A.E.C. general manager, tried to make Tamplin criticize Sternglass but delete his risk estimate of 4,000 fatalities. Even though this was a mere fraction of Sternglass' estimate, the A.E.C. executives did not want to lend credence to the Pittsburgh scientist's report. When Tamplin refused to accede to the telephone pressure from Washington, Totter wrote two letters reiterating his demands.

Tamplin defied his superiors and published the complete paper as a technical document. As A.E.C. pressure built up, Tamplin got together with his Livermore laboratory colleague John Gofman, and they decided to fight back. The two men, who bear a resemblance to the Smith Brothers of cough drop fame, began their attack with a San Francisco speech in October 1969. They called for a tenfold cut in allowable radiation levels and argued that permissible radiation-exposure levels could lead to an excess 32,000 cancers annually. The following month they reiterated their demand before the Senate Public Works Subcommittee on Air and Water Pollution. They argued that the Federal Radiation Council and the International Council on Radiation Protection, which sets the national and international exposure standards were not properly concerned with public health. As evidence they presented statements by the I.C.R.P. that revealed some of the basic criteria used to establish radiation safety guidelines:

"There is a great value in simplicity in administrative rules, if they are to be obeyed and if an unacceptable burden is not to be placed on those responsible for seeing that the recommendations are carried out. This almost certainly will imply some degree of compromise for risk-based recommendations. . . . It is evident that at the present time risk considerations [the chances of getting cancer] can at best play only a very general role in specific recommendations such as those for non-nuclear exposure and that operational and administrative convenience must of necessity often be of equal importance."

In December 1969 the A.E.C. staff in Washington issued a nine-page critique of the renegade scientists' call for tougher radiation standards. The agency said there was nothing new in the Gofman-Tamplin paper, that the data were inconclusive and the report should have been published in a respectable, refereed scientific journal before it was released to Congress (this is the line the A.E.C. used unsuccessfully to persuade Tamplin to delete his risk estimate in the Sternglass critique). Later the A.E.C. officials added that they were unable to make a strong public refutation of the Gofman-Tamplin charges because it would be necessary to counter their clear-cut conclusions with dull, meticulous scientific data.

But the Federal Radiation Council, which set the nation's radiation protection standards, disagreed with the A.E.C. On January 28, 1970, the council revealed that it was initiating an unprecedented review of radiation standards as called for by Gofman and Tamplin. Instead of honoring the two critics, the scientific establishment snubbed them. On January 30, 1970, Phillip Abelson, editor of influential *Science* magazine, co-discoverer of neptunium and a charter member of the nuclear-power fan club, rejected a Gofman-Tamplin paper on the need for tighter radiation standards. Then, in early February, *Science* published a three-page critique of the Gofman-Tamplin report.

Late in 1970 the Federal Radiation Council was taken over by the Environmental Protection Agency, which appointed six committees to make the task-force study on the standards. Four of the committees were with the National Academy of Sciences, one was a federal interagency panel, and one was the National Council on Radiation Protection and Measurement. The six groups were to report to the E.P.A. by July 1972 and a final decision on the radiation-exposure standards was expected by the end of 1972.

In January 1971 the N.C.R.P. became the first of the six committees to make clear its view on the standards question. This group, which has provided the scientific basis for radiation-control standards in the U. S. since 1929, reported that current standards were basically safe. The membership of the N.C.R.P. included such men as Cincinnati radiologist Eugene Saenger, who is doing vital studies on radiation exposure for the Defense Nuclear Agency (see Chapter 5). In fact, 31 of the 64 members of the N.C.R.P. were directly employed or had their research supported by the A.E.C., the Pentagon, General Electric and Westinghouse (the two manufacturers of nuclear-power stations).

But Gofman and Tamplin, who refused to stay on the A.E.C. team, found their support diminishing. Tamplin's budget was cut from 300,000 dollars to 70,000 dollars, reducing his 12-man staff to one. Tamplin claimed this was reprisal, but the agency claimed it was merely the result of a fund shortage. For a time the A.E.C. compounded Tamplin's problem by routinely refusing travel funds to speak to groups worried about radioactive pollution. When he relied on independent financing for his trips, Tamplin returned home to find his pay docked for each travel day.

In July 1970 Ralph Nader mentioned this to Senator Edmund Muskie, who wrote A.E.C. Chairman Seaborg about it. Seaborg agreed to initiate a staff review that concluded that Tamplin had not been discriminated against. Muskie replied that he did not feel the A.E.C.'s study was necessarily impartial and asked for the American Association for the Advancement of Science (A.A.A.S.) to make an independent investigation of the problem. In September Dr. Gofman wrote Seaborg asking for a restoration of Tamplin's budget and staff. Seaborg replied that he would defer decision on this until after the A.A.A.S. responded to Muskie's request. At the end of December 1970 the A.A.A.S. board of directors voted to make an investigation of the Gofman-Tamplin affair. A few days later Dr. Seaborg was swept in as president-elect of the A.A.A.S. The A.E.C. chairman swore, however, that he would not interfere with the A.A.A.S. investigation of the Gofman-Tamplin case.

CHAPTER TEN

CONCLUSION

The conscientious American citizen of the 1970s finds himself beset with more crises than he could surmount in a dozen lifetimes. There is the housing crisis, the school crisis and the traffic crisis. Such simple acts as the purchase of a week's groceries, fumigating a pear tree or driving to work are bound up in numerous ecological, nutritional and biological quandaries. The dedicated legislator must be a walking encyclopedia conversant with such matters as sideline noise, monosodium glutamate and hydrocarbon emissions. But in this age of social anxiety and environmentalism, nuclear weapons are a decidedly second-rate issue. The voluminous handbook for the 1970 environmental teach-in carried not a single word about radiation pollution.

Certain groups such as the Committee for a Sane Nuclear Policy have successfully lobbied for such things as the atmospheric nuclear-test ban. The Colorado Committee for Environmental Information has publicized the dangers at Rocky Flats. Scientists such as John Gofman, Arthur Tamplin and Edward Martell, crusaders such as Leo Goodman and writers such as Paul Jacobs and Ralph Lapp have also fought to protect the public interest against the weapons program. But the public has failed to perceive the nuclear-weapons business as more than a periodic threat. When everyone gets uptight about fallout, the A.E.C. cancels atmospheric tests. If Rocky Flats burns, the agency insists that future precautions will eliminate all hazard. If a Nevada test vents, experts assure the public this was a rare accident that won't happen again. Because the radiation from these accidents is virtually imperceptible to the senses, the A.E.C. can escape public concern again and again. Only the best specialist will be able to discern the latent effects and his testimony will doubtless be refuted by the agency's hand-picked flak catchers.

In the fall of 1971 Alaska Senator Mike Gravel was leading a big campaign against an underground shot called CANNIKIN at the agency's supplemental test site on Amchitka Island, Alaska. But even if this, America's largest underground nuclear test, were blocked, it would only be a small beginning to the end of our weapons program. For since the atmospheric-test-ban treaty, the rate of nuclear-weapons testing has actually increased. Between July 1945 and August 1963 the United States, Russia, Great Britain and France averaged 24 tests a year. From the signing of the test-ban treaty to the end of 1970 there was an average of 42 tests a year. During the first nine months of 1970 the United States announced 23 underground tests versus six by the Russians.

Clearly the forces that have mobilized against CANNIKIN must widen their focus if they expect to stop the A.E.C. and the Pentagon. These agencies are too experienced at thwarting piecemeal protest. America needs a mass movement working on the assumption that the mere existence of a nuclear-weapons program is a strategic liability. The care and feeding of 40,000 nuclear weapons endangers the lives of the workers and the public. Nuclear weapons also imperil the national defense, because an enemy could strike a mortal blow merely by hitting one of our numerous stockpiles and scattering toxic radionuclides over our cities. For example, a strike on Albuquerque's Manzano base, Denver's Rocky Flats or Amarillo's Pantex plant would release enough nuclear material to necessitate evacuation and possible condemnation of the region.

Our entire nuclear-defense system is predicated on assumptions that belie common sense. Take antimissiles, which are supposed to intercept enemy nuclear weapons before they reach their American targets. If one of these antimissiles should intercept a Soviet missile over New York City, the resulting explosion would release toxic plutonium in the New York area. The same holds true if we knock out an enemy bomber. The result is serious contamination of our own neighborhood. At a minimum, Palomares-style cleanups would be necessary, and at worst, this nuclear material would void large sections of the American landscape in much the same way the Nevada test site is now a no-man's-land.

There are other serious limitations to nuclear warfare. Dr. Herbert York, who headed the Livermore Laboratory and the Pentagon's Research and Engineering Divison during the 1950s and early 1960s, has had a hand in building many nuclear weapons and believes some would doubtless fail. Dr. York is doubtful about the reliability of nuclear warheads stored in silos for years under elaborate precautions designed to preclude accidental detonation. Suddenly at combat time these dormant weapons must be armed and ready to go at the right millisecond. This sort of hair-trigger reliability is not something we can count on and is one reason Dr. York opposed building the ABM. And when the nuclear weapon is fired, there is an added risk that it might abort on the launching pad and scatter radioactive debris around populated areas. A related problem is an errant missile that could strike our own country or neutral neighbors such as Mexico and Canada. The A.E.C.'s Dr. Tamplin believes these neutral countries might well take some of the worst fallout damage.

These are some of the reasons experts tell us no one could survive a nuclear war or, at best, the living would envy the dead. But when these same experts are cornered into explaining how to dismantle the nuclear arsenal, they lapse into talk of bilateral disarmament, i.e., the SALT talks or the Geneva negotiations. The idea is that America must sit down with the other nuclear powers and jointly dispose of nuclear weapons. But this sort of talk has gone on for over a decade and produced only an atmospheric-test ban plus some accords about not stationing nuclear weapons in outer space and under the sea. No headway has been made on actually dismantling the nuclear arsenal or curbing the rate of testing. At the same time our SALT negotiatiors are trying to stop nuclear-weapons development, the nuclear architects in the A.E.C. are embarked on the largest weapons-production program in American history to ready the ABM. The CANNIKIN test has been planned as the biggest underground detonation ever. The beleagured Rocky Flats facility is doubling capacity and employment is soaring to an all-time high. The A.E.C. is expanding the weapons business on every front. The hawks are told new facilities are needed to meet weapons demand and the doves are told improvements will make the nuclear business safer.

How can anyone believe America cares about disarmament when it is boosting the weapons program to new production peaks? How can anyone trust American disarmament negotiators when the weapons makers are willing to lie to their workers and the public about the safety of these nuclear devices? Who, studying the record of deceit, lying, coverups, censorship, reprisals and intimidation, could trust these bomb men? The fires, explosions, criticality accidents, contamination incidents, fallout catastrophes, underground test ventings, miner fatalities, indoor radon seepage, waste-disposal mishaps and nuclear-bomber crashes were not the work of some sinister enemy but our own government, which professes to protect us.

It is a familiar tale to anyone who has dealt with big government. Americans who read newspapers or watch televison are perpetually reminded that bureaucrats are more concerned about the image of their nonhuman agencies than about the public welfare. The Forest Service permits forests to be slashed for toilet paper and then burns down quaint ghost towns as fire hazards. The director of the F.B.I. puts a wiretap on his former boss, the attorney general. The C.I.A. makes and wrecks foreign governments and the details are glamorized by television serials. The Agriculture Department subsidizes farms owned by wealthy senators and ignores those owned by the poor. The Food and Drug Administration is an industry front and the Bureau of Mines works for the mine owners, not the miners. So no one can profess surprise when he finds out that the Atomic Energy Commission or the Pentagon is making its share of mistakes with the nuclear-weapons program.

If they were regulating Permapress fabric or ten-speed bicycles, perhaps the collective negligence could be overlooked. But in the nuclear-weapons business there can be no room for error. They are dealing with long-lived radionuclides that will be potentially lethal for thousands of years. The genetic consequences of their malfeasance are infinite. Americans may have the right to annihilate themselves with these nuclear poisons, but this license to kill does not extend to future generations.

This is why the men in the nuclear-weapons business must be judged more carefully than their counterparts in other federal agencies. Their record over the past 25 years inspires a vote of no confidence. We can't continue to trust these men who are unable to predict the wind for an atmospheric test. We can't trust these men who are out illicitly burying plutonium in a metropolitan area. We can't let them continue to build bombs in factories that can't withstand hailstorms. The mad nuclear bombers must be stopped.

Presented with this verdict, the government would probably appoint some sort of federal commission that would suggest some vague reforms, perhaps some new filters for Rocky Flats, deeper holes for the Nevada test site or a new firewall at Pantex. An alternative would be to change the administrative structure of the weapons program. The Nixon administration has, in fact, suggested the weapons-production complex might do a better job if it were run by the Pentagon instead of by the A.E.C. But reform is no solution, because the same experts would go on making the same mistakes for a different employer.

The sole practical solution is unilateral disarmament. This means that the great American bomb machine should be condemned as an acute public-health hazard to the nation. The bombs should all be called in, dismantled and buried under the supervision of competent authorities. The entire operation should be conducted without secrecy and be independently reviewed by experts who have no official connection with the weapons program.

Dismantling the weapons program involves certain priorities. The first is an immediate shutdown of the Rocky Flats plant outside Denver. All fissionable material should be safely buried at a remote nuclear dump. The plant itself should be cemented in and put under permanent radiological surveillance. Ground crews, perhaps under the direction of Dr. Martell, should immediately begin a comprehensive soil survey of land around the plant, pinpoint the radioactive hot spots and bury the contaminated soil in licensed dumps.

The second priority is termination of all nuclear tests. Dr. York, the former Livermore Laboratory chief, believes cancellation of underground tests would help spur worldwide disarmament. After the test program is cancelled, the Nevada test site and the supplemental test site on Amchitka should be closed. The Nevada site should be given comprehensive radiological surveillance to find the plutonium hot spots, which should be scooped up and buried. The test site should be kept under permanent surveillance and closed to the public forever.

Next the government should shut down all stockpile sites worldwide and bring the weapons to Pantex and Burlington, where they would be dismantled. The work might be done under the direction of a competent authority such as Dr. Martell or Dr. York. Afterwards, the two factories should be shut down.

Then the Colorado plateau should be declared a national disaster area, with accelerated radiological surveillance of all homes built on mill tailings. Homes found to be over the danger level should be either moved or dismantled with compensation to the owners paid by the federal government. All tailings piles should be put under a federally financed independent authority that would take charge of permanent stabilization. Deep-water-well disposal of tailings should be halted and all uranium mines should be shut down until they can operate at the 0.3 working level.

The A.E.C.'s Division of Military Affairs, the Defense Nuclear Agency and all other Pentagon agencies working in the nuclear-weapons business should be closed down. This would mean terminating all weapons-design functions at Los Alamos and Livermore, closing down the Sandia laboratories and all other plants in the production complex. The nuclear-weapons school, the nuclear research and all other phases of the program should be halted.

Dr. Glenn T. Seaborg should resign the chairmanship of the Atomic Energy Commission. On June 3, 1955, Dr. Seaborg was paid 100,000 dollars by the American government for his work on the plutonium separative process used to manufacture the Nagasaki bomb. This pioneering work was done by Seaborg and three colleagues at the University of California in Berkeley during 1940 and 1941. Seaborg and his friends made inventions and discoveries pertaining to plutonium and its isotopes, particularly plutonium 239 and its neutron fissionability as well as its chemical properties. The work included the discovery that plutonium in its lower oxidation state is carried from solution by certain precipitates, whereas in the higher oxidation state it is not carried. Subsequently Seaborg and his colleagues were engaged in work under the Office of Scientific Research and Development and the Manhattan District, where they made valuable contributions to the ultimate production of the Nagasaki weapon.

These early inventions and discoveries on the plutonium separative process for the Nagasaki weapon became the subject matter of classified patent applications filed by the scientists between 1945 and 1947. They filed application for award before the A.E.C.'s Patent Compensation Board on January 8, 1950. On June 3, 1955, each of the four men was given 100,000 dollars for release of all claims against the government and assignment to the A.E.C. of all right, title and interest in the inventions subsequently published under patents number 2,908,621; 3,000,695; 3,000,697; and 3,190,804.

Any man capable of drawing 100,000 dollars for his work on the Nagasaki weapon, which took tens of thousands of lives, has no business chairing the Atomic Energy Commission let alone the American Association for the Advancement of Science.

Dismantling the weapons program and deposing the weapons makers is not the end. The federal government should immediately set up a compensation apparatus for all those who have lost their jobs until they can find nonnuclear-weapons employment. There should be a comprehensive epidemiological study of the occupational and ecological effects of the weapons program. Drs. Gofman and Tamplin would be competent to head such a study. Among areas of special interest are the health of all people who have ever worked at Rocky Flats or the Nevada and South Pacific test sites. Epidemiological studies should also focus on these three areas. Declassification of all weapons-program records should expedite this work. Occupational victims of the weapons program, particularly the miners, should be compensated by the federal government.

Unilateral disarmament is the only way for America to get rid of the weapons program. America started this insane nuclear race and America should be the first to end it. But the demolition job should not put an end to the history of this American tragedy. The Sandia Museum in Albuquerque should be expanded. Special rooms should be set up with photographic displays of the victims at Hiroshima and Nagasaki. Films should tell the tragic story of the Nevada test site and Rocky Flats. Palomares and Thule should rate a special section. The indoor-radon and tailings story should be charted and mapped. Maybe the A.E.C.'s Brookhaven Laboratory might pickle a few of the poisoned thyroids removed from the Rongelap natives and put them on display. Perhaps a monument could commemorate the uranium miners who died through official negligence. And maybe Dr. Seaborg would dig back through his 1955 archives and find that cancelled 100,000-dollar check for his fine work on the Nagasaki weapon. It could be laminated and hung in the Sandia museum right above Fat Man.

On July 21, 1971, after this book had gone to press, Chairman Glenn T. Seaborg resigned from the Atomic Energy Commission to return to academic life at the University of California. He was succeeded by 42-year-old James R. Schlesinger who had been assistant director of the Office of Management and Budget. President Richard M. Nixon told Seaborg that he accepted his resignation with special regret: "As a world-famous chemist, scholar and administrator you have contributed in a unique and meaningful way to far greater understanding and application of the miracles of the atom."